My Inner Life, the Animals and the Angels

Helena Hawley

My Inner Life, the Animals and the Angels

©2000 Helena Hawley

ISBN 186163 121 9

Cover and internal illustrations by Helena Hawley
Cover design by Paul Mason

Published by:

Capall Bann Publishing
Freshfields
Chieveley
Berks
RG20 8TF

Dedication

I dedicate this book to my beloved and beautiful horse
"Wilderness"
who has given me so much pleasure and service over the years
that I have known him.

Also by Helena Hawley, published by Capall Bann:

*The Other Kingdoms Speak - What the Animals, Plants, Crystals,
Extraterrestrials, Angels, Mermaids & Fairies Have to Say*

Acknowledgements

I acknowledge the help and support that has come to me from so many beings both incarnate and discarnate in the writing of this book. I include those who encouraged me to keep writing it, and not least Patrick Kempe who supported the project in his role as distant healer, and those who generously allowed me to write about their past lives as animals. I thank Jill Robinson for her hard work proof-reading the manuscript, and for her kindness in providing me with the preface.

After completing the first few chapters of this book, I lost all inclination to write any more, even though I knew it was part of my mission. At first I secretly and wrongly blamed my boyfriend, but when we split up for other reasons during my non-writing period, I discovered that even without him, I could not bring myself to want to write. He was not to blame. I wondered what could be done to help me regain my enthusiasm.

When Gila and Michael Galitzine invited me to join their wonderful workshop in Germany at the end of 1994 called "Reise in die Zukunft", or "Journey into the Future", free of charge, I took it as a sign that this was part of my pathway. Although I had no idea what this would bring me, I accepted this generous gift from them, and aside from the wonderful 'Journey into the Future', the work on my chakra system totally transformed me. I discovered that my throat chakra was quite blocked, and this is the energy centre that governs self-expression and communication, my creativity was literally stuck inside me and could not flow. After I arrived home, I found that I was full of the desire to write again. Even though time did not permit it just then, this stayed with me until time and opportunity came together again, whereupon I was able to enthusiastically and joyfully continue with this book. Thank you Gila and Michael.

My biggest thank you goes to Linda TellingtonJones for her continued support and friendship, and finding time in an impossibly busy schedule that most of us could never cope with to write the First Preface for this book.

Contents

First Preface

Helena Hawley has opened a magical door into the animal kingdom in the spirit world. Few who have been honoured with such communication have the courage or perseverance to speak of their experiences or publish them. It was over a decade ago when Helena first told me of a message she had received from a horse in a week long training I was teaching. I felt the information was important to our entire group, and urged her to share it. When she did, with much trepidation, she discovered that the message was indeed life-changing to several participants in the training.

Subsequently, other spirit animals began to enter her meditation, often species previously unknown to her. Over time, as though the word spread throughout the spirit world of animals, many came to her, often with disturbing words of woe.

When Helena had collected messages from a wide variety of animals, she showed them to me. I was immediately struck with the thought that a major piece was missing - the story of her personal journey. Her courage in sharing this in her first book has been a valuable gift to opening doors to new worlds.

Almost two decades ago, while visiting Michael Roads in Australia, a thousand year old Morton Bay fig tree graced me with the following message:

"In order to re-balance or realign the earth, your people must once again recognise the kingdoms of the plants, the animals, the minerals and the nature spirits as One with you, and as vital to the survival of the planet. That your race recognise the God within is only the start. That we are recognised as One with you is the key - not only to survival -but to Heaven on Earth."

7

In this book, Helena's second, she takes us on a magical journey into the secret worlds of mermaids and fairies and extraterrestrials. As you share her experiences, may doors into these dimensions open to you with a heightened awareness and clarity, and enrich your life with new appreciation and understanding.

Linda Tellington-Jones

Preface

I first met Helena Hawley at the first "Annual Dolphin Tribe Gathering" held on the Island of Maui, Hawaii, in June 1996. Over lunch, one day towards the end of our week together, I overheard Helena mentioning that on her return to England she needed to find someone to proof-read her second book. Somewhat to my amazement I heard myself volunteering to undertake this task, and when I received the manuscript I knew why, as it is one of the, if not *the* most remarkable book I have had the good fortune to read.

If I had read it without first having met Helena, I might have been inclined to dismiss it as the work of someone with a very active and vivid imagination. However, having spent time in Helena's company, I feel that she is a person of high integrity, and therefore that this book is a sincere and faithful record of some of the spiritual adventures she has been privileged to enjoy, and of the messages which she feels she has been entrusted to pass on to her brothers and sisters currently incarnating on Planet Earth at this critical time in our evolution.

I hope that Helena's work will inspire you as much as it has me, for I feel encouraged to continue with my own spiritual development in the knowledge that more help is now available to assist us in this transformative process.

Jill Robinson
Spiritual Healer
England
August, 1996.

Pre-Introduction

For those who did not read Book One

Book One, *"The Other Kingdoms Speak"*, is the complete preparation for Book Two. Published by Capall Bann Publishing in England, it has a lengthy introduction in which I describe the ups and downs of my early life, and how I was gradually brought to understand that it is part of my mission as a lightworker to share the messages and knowledge that I receive from the other kingdoms with the rest of humanity.

I am not special, for there are many light-workers on the planet at the moment. We are here to work together to increase the level of awareness of people as the transition into the Age of Aquarius, or New Age takes place.

The teachings or messages that I can offer are the ones I have learnt or been given myself.

Book One describes the sometimes painful, sometimes joyful stages of my own personal development starting with the trials of being a misunderstood child who did not understand herself or others, progressing through life as an isolated and damaged adult who resorted to alcohol when seeking relief from pain, to the more aware person who with much help from many friends re-emerged as a happier person with a purpose in life, and something to give. The animals, trees, crystals, angels, fairies, mermaids and other life-forms all played their part in my healing. The animals (in spirit form) came first, introduced themselves to an astonished me as the Council of Animals and told me that as I had almost got over my fear of people, I was nearly ready to work with them. This unexpected acceptance from them touched and opened my heart. My gift to them is sharing these experiences with the world. You will find more about The Council of Animals in this book. The mermaids in Book One had a hard time with me, because I felt so confident that they did not exist, but just wait until you get to Book Three!!

The simple nature of those early channellings makes them easy for the reader to follow. This simplicity is still present in Book Two, but I have become more daring with the nature of the things that I am willing to share. It is a sequel to Book One, and a stepping-stone to Book Three which I have not yet put together, although I have already collected some exciting material for it.

Now for Book Two...

Introduction

I was talking on the telephone to distant healer Patrick Kempe on January 8th. 1994 about the health of my mother, my horse, and me (I had had back problems), when quite out of the blue Patrick said, "Are you still writing books?" I was a little taken back by the sudden change of subject, especially as although I had mentioned having written one some months previously, this had never seemed a relevant topic of conversation with him before. I explained at length why not much was happening at that time, and finished with the words, "...since you asked." Patrick flatly denied having asked anything about books, but when I insisted that a voice which was definitely not mine, and sounded just like his had said very clearly on the telephone "Are you still writing books?" he admitted that sometimes one of his spiritual guides will talk through him without him realising it, and added that "In that case it means that you ought to be writing one, and you have got enough material there." When I thought about it, I believed this, and realised that the magic moment had come to start preparing a second book. In my mind, I called it "Book Two."

It is my wish that by sharing the animal messages, these teachings which have been given to me, and some more of my own spiritual journey, that readers will feel nourished and less alone while experiencing life on Earth in a physical body.

Although there are happy people about, it is not uncommon for life to include suffering in various degrees either in childhood, or adulthood or both. These experiences increase our capacity for compassion very often, for we come to understand so much better the suffering of others, but it can also have the negative result that we cut ourselves off from the people around us, and learn to avoid the intensity of our own emotions. It is part of a survival technique which I indulged in almost all the time some years ago, but when I was ready to recognise what a poor sort of half existence this was, and consciously choose to find an alternative way of being, on 5th. September 1982, a prayer in the form of a poem was channelled to me from my spiritual guides.

> *"Wrap me in an amber cloak*
> *To thaw my frozen heart*
> *Put me in a golden boat*
> *To sail out from the dark*
> *Let the Light I have within*
> *Seek the Light without*
> *And may the love that's in my heart*
> *Touch people round about."*

This to me sums up so much of what life is about. 'Light' can be interpreted as Light, God, Spirit, or consciousness. Which ever of these I pick, I recognise that it is something that exists in all of creation.

Especially in the West separation is well understood, but no longer appropriate for homo-sapiens who are so separate and out of touch with Nature, that most of them are steadily but surely continuing to destroy and pollute the Planet.

Many people are becoming aware of a desperate need to reconnect with the rest of consciousness, (seek the Light without) and this book of my sharings is offered to help such souls to open their awareness to the rest of consciousness.

In the hope that my heart has defrosted a little since 1982, I open myself to you, and bring you these writings in love.

Helena.

Chapter 1

The Council of Animals

Following Patrick Kempe's gentle nudge to proceed with another book, I set about the preparation for it. Before opening myself to inspiration with my word processor, or feeling ready to sit and meditate, I felt it to be necessary to prepare my house and my life and me. In spite of a flurry of activity in my daily life with very little time at home, I set about cleaning the house, answering post, clearing out cupboards, and very important, discarding anything I could find that I no longer needed. These procedures created the space for new creativity, a new project. It also meant that I could concentrate on a book without thinking about the other jobs that needed doing. Nonetheless, it was only when the weather turned to frost and snow that I really saw my opportunity to begin in earnest, for the work with the horses that normally keeps me out of the house was systematically cancelled each breakfast time by incoming telephone calls from disappointed clients, who rightly felt that their precious animals should not be asked to work on the hard and/or slippery ground..

As it was the messages from the animals that inspired me to write my first book, it seems appropriate to introduce "The Council of Animals" in the very first chapter. They have not finished speaking, either as a group, or as individual members. I also wish to introduce Margot, a friend who successfully persuaded me to allow her to come to my house to meditate for half an hour approximately once a month. I was very reluctant, as I was not sure if I would be able to get my usual type of material through with someone present who might not be able to accept either what I received or me as I am if she knew what I was really like. Therefore I gave her a rough copy of my first book to browse through, telling her that if she was still interested after that, I would consider it. "...but you ought to know more about me first," I explained. Well that did not put her off. So I welcomed her, and had no idea what a gift I was allowing myself. Not only was she to be a friend to me, but her coming meant that I had to discipline myself to meditate which made it easier for the animals and others to get a word in. It was at home in Margot's quiet presence that the Council of Animals chose to appear on 7th. February 1994.

At the beginning of the meditation I saw an angel-being with a clearly visible halo and surrounded by light. The angel appeared to be praying for me with great fervour. I also felt myself touched on the forehead and at the back of my neck, just around the place where tension tends to build up, and I experienced this as receiving healing.

I waited for a while to see what would happen next, and as nothing happened, I decided to give my meditation some direction, and asked if there was anything I should know about "Book Two".

A picture of a beautifully bound black book with gold around the edges of its pages like a bible, and "Book Two" written in gold on the front of it appeared before my eyes. From behind it came three or four enormous elephants. When I asked if they were going to have something to do with "Book Two", the largest one trumpeted with a roaring shriek, which I gathered meant "yes". Telepathically I realised that along with various other life forms, the elephants have walked the Earth for a very long time, and as I began to link up with the rest of the Animal Council, I felt a deep concern amongst them for Planet Earth which they loved so well. I had wondered if only the elephants were present, but as I looked around I saw a giraffe with its head towering up amongst the tree tops, then others such as a rhinoceros, a tiger, a cobra, (the first time that I had seen one of those), birds of prey, insects, and then I knew without looking further that I was in the middle of a complete circle of animal life. Speaking with one voice, I clearly heard them say,

"You are a child in our garden."

I saw myself looking very small (child-sized) sitting on the ground in the centre of a large clearing. Well away from me around its perimeters were tall trees and the animals.

"MAN IS THE WORST PEST ON THE PLANET."

The voice speaking was deep and powerful.

"We have been pushed aside to the perimeters of man's expanding civilizations. At one time we were to be found almost everywhere, but now mankind in the name of progress has taken almost all of our territory from us, and polluted the Planet so badly that even his own existence is seriously threatened. We realise that we are referring to the majority, and that there also exists a loving and caring minority, but we need a majority vote from mankind. The majority to whom we have referred is so taken with greed, technological progress, and material wealth, that they are determinedly blind to the untold damage and suffering that they cause to Earthly Creation; that is to all life forms including the planet itself."

The next part was more about the nature of the animal kingdom, and the Animal Council, and how the two are connected. It was explained to me that in most cases, the part of Consciousness (God, or Spirit if you like) which incarnates into the animal kingdom, has chosen simply to be here in physical form experiencing life as it comes, and living according to the inherent instincts and development of each individual species. Mostly they just are. Some of the more evolved ones have powerful emotional bodies, which is why when we keep them as captives, there is much more than just their physical welfare to think about. Although their different individual qualities and wisdom are sadly underestimated by mankind most of the time, this "living according to instincts" and just "being" on the Earth makes the existence of the Council of Animals an essential part of their welfare and future evolution. It was hoped that more of those in contact with mankind would benefit from the connection with a more advanced form of consciousness, but mostly the reverse with countless mis-understandings has been the case. (This is excluding the good and caring minority of people.) There is still time to improve our relationship with their kingdom, for we are here to experience many things, and we are gifted with the free-will to make changes. The Animals are pressing for these changes.

The Council of Animals is a body acting as guardian angels for the animal kingdom. They are a very conscious counter-part watching over the development and fate of the animals on this planet. I perceived a white silvery coloured mist shining down from the Council of Animals to the animal life forms on our planet. The Council seeks to help both the animals and mankind by opening our eyes to the effects of our behaviour here, and the destruction that we cause, which brings with it a heavy karmic debt for our human species.

I felt the intensity of the feelings behind the words that the Council had given me, but it was not simply anger, it was a longing for understanding and recognition. I felt a great sadness coming from them, and as the animals started to walk out from under the trees into the clearing, I saw tears running down their faces. They were moving towards me before dispersing, but all I could think about at that point was how hard it was going to be for me to accurately record and remember the information given to me so far with its strange new concepts. Also it was heavy material, and really I had had enough for one night, so I asked to be lifted out of it and taken away to something lighter. I was thankful for what I had received.

This was not the first visit of the Council, but it was definitely the clearest explanation of what it is and its purpose that I have been given. Representatives of individual species have also been and spoken to me, and what they have had to say you will read later.

Chapter 2
The Nature of Consciousness

Consciousness to me has a very fluid nature, and is as flexible as water. It can divide, or come together. Its size and shape is not fixed. As Helena, I can have more of it or less of it, and the part of it that I currently call mine likes to travel and move freely. It does not choose to remain tightly bound to the physical body. In addition, a part of me with the ability to recall events and sensations is frequently in attendance on these journeys, so I have memories of experiencing some remarkable things.

I choose to illustrate this point with a story about a fish experience, and then various discoveries made with the help of a tree, including something about the nature of the tree consciousness.

A Fish

It was about the beginning of July 1989 as I slipped into a meditative state that I found myself experiencing life from the inside of a fish. In effect, I was the fish. Imagination? I discounted that possibility, as although now I could imagine it with great difficulty, at the time I would not have known how it felt to be a fish. I have no idea what species of fish it was, but I saw myself as quite a large fish with a fairly large mouth. I was silvery coloured underneath, and bluey-grey on top. All of my scales glistened causing me to shine a bit like so many other fish. I was swimming about in the midst of a shoal of similar fish. Although I felt as if I swam freely in whichever direction I wanted to, and the other fish likewise, there was never any chance of a collision. Avoiding each other was something that seemed to occur quite naturally without

19

any effort on the part of the fish. This astonished me, as walking in a crowd as a human, I am one of the worst at not bumping into everyone else.

My tail was very powerful, and with effortless skill I used it to propel myself through the water in an incredibly efficient and co-ordinated way, which is very alien to my unco-ordinated human endeavours. It was this last point that convinced me that it was totally beyond my powers to invent such an experience.

In the Forest

Three years on in late August, I had gone out for a long hike in a large forest belonging to the Forestry Commission. Consequently most of its paths were well used as the trees there are periodically harvested, and then replaced with tiny saplings which will in turn years later also be cut down. However, in the very centre of the forest while walking down a path that was very little used, where nothing had been disturbed for a long time, and the peace of a late Summer evening soothed my consciousness, I felt moved to stop and connect with one of the trees. The forest here was so exceptionally still and quiet, that I could easily have believed that the rest of humanity lived one hundred miles away at the very closest. Nothing ever passed this way to disturb the peace. The trees were growing silently.

I reached out with a hand and gently grasped the nearest bit of pine tree as I closed my eyes. I became aware of energy moving through my body. It rose up from the Earth, passed through my feet working its way up to my head. I could also sense the same energy pulsating upwards from the ground and passing with its regular steady vibration through the tree. Just to check that this really was so, I tried letting go of the tree, and found that the energy was of the earth, not of the tree, as it continued to travel through my body. However, when I did link up with the tree it was stronger.

It was the first time that I had walked in this place, and yet it seemed to me that I had met all of the trees and the heather and vibrations and everything else before. I was familiar with being alone with myself in remote places such as this, but why did all trees, woods, and wild places give off vibrations that were in part similar no matter in which area of the planet I found them?

The answer came through the tree. All trees were part of the tree consciousness. They all shared this link with one another, and they were all connected to the Earth who supported them, and gave them life on as many areas of her surface as she was able and permitted to. The trees responded with their beneficial effects on the ecology of the planet.

I became curious about this energy which rose up continuously from the centre of the Earth, through her outer crust, travelling through the tree and me and anything else that was there. Surely at some stage the Earth would run out of energy to send away? Then I saw clairvoyantly how she had pores in her crust through which she could breath. In some places energy came out, and in others she could take new energy into herself. I saw pictures of the energies surrounding the Earth. They entered her atmosphere from space. These extra-terrestrial energies were very powerful, many originating from various other planets. Not all of their influences were desirable. Some were good, and others appeared like dark shadows sweeping towards her. It was not necessary that they harm the Earth, however, as I perceived a narrow band of golden light gradually building up like a fiery aura around her, and I sensed her as a conscious being who had made the decision to choose the light from the darkness. Thanking the tree for its connection with me, I moved on.

Chapter 3

Power in Unity

I am not using chronological order of events in the chapters of this book, but allowing things to enter into it in harmony with the energy flow that I feel inside me as I open myself to inspiration for this work. This brings me to a teaching I received in meditation at home on 14th. April 1989.

I saw two angels who I took to be my guides, one in pale blue, and the other in creamy-white. Other discarnate beings in various pastel shades joined us. It may have been the creamy-white guide who asked, "Ready for take-off?" I thought that this must mean that we were going to visit another planet, as that is what had happened several times previously, but I was wrong as you will see. It was at this moment that I was warned that afterwards I must write down everything that took place. I agreed, and said that I was ready.

There must have been about six beings visibly present other than my guides. I saw a ring of bright lilac light of about two to three foot in diameter. Each of the other beings reached up and held the light with one hand. I watched from outside their circle, and felt that I was supposed to be participating in this somehow. Therefore I put myself in the middle of the circle only to be fished out of it immediately by the cream-coloured guide. That had obviously been a beginner's error!

I was then shown a gap in the circle, and encouraged to take my place in it and hold the lilac light-ring like the others. I wanted to know if we were going to give healing to Planet Earth, or was the light-ring too small to fit round it? In answer to my thoughts I was shown how the dimensions could adapt themselves to suit our wishes, and the light-ring which had taken on a pinker colour was now surrounding the Earth.

I began to survey my immediate surroundings, and I saw that alongside us many angels were flying around the Earth. I was told that they were infiltrating the atmosphere, although mostly fairly high up, in order to bring their love and light to it, and in this way help the transmutation of all consciousness on the planet. (Including the raising of consciousness.)

After this the light-ring returned to its previous size some distance away from the Earth in the place where we had started. One of the things that intrigued me about it now was the way in which it changed colour. It went through shades of soft green, gold, blue, and lilac. I never actually saw it change, but it was as though after I had blinked or cast a glance at something else, I looked back and noted the new colour.

As we held the ring, we did not have our feet on any firm ground, but were simply dangling from it in space. I noticed something very interesting. As I hung there and relaxed, (not hard, for I was weightless), our bodies fell together and became one, while there was a similar blending of our consciousness. We became the consciousness and the light surrounding the light-ring. As this happened, my personal identity disappeared. Although I felt it must be somewhere, it had temporarily vanished. I was no longer being me. I was no one at all, and at the same time I was the whole of the six or seven of us hanging from the ring. This was a good feeling. I felt secure in it, and saw that our light was at least three times as strong with this blending than it had been when we were separate. I felt completely comfortable in it, whereas before I had been feeling that I was a human-being in the midst of many other kinds of beings. In fact I had been questioning whether or not I really belonged with the others.

Finally we landed somewhere, and sat in a little circle as separate entities again. There was much light there, and the light-ring, which was lilac-coloured again was hovering just above us.

For me this was really a lesson in "the power of unity", the increase in potential power when individuals come together for a single purpose, of security in unity, of the beauty in uniting with the consciousness of other types of being, for I did not feel human vibrations from the other beings involved, yet their consciousness was totally compatible with mine. The significance is that when we as humans connect with the consciousness of the animals or nature, it is a perfectly natural and beautiful procedure. There is no need to fear the loss of one's personal identity, for that represents separation, the quality currently reigning in excess on the Earth, the cause of great disharmony. We are better off without it.

Chapter 4

Gut Ising

Gut Ising is situated close to the banks of Lake Chiemsee in southern Germany, where there are some beautiful forests. It was the venue for a clinic led by Linda Tellington-Jones, the Canadian born animal trainer and healer from the States, where a group of us (already trained in her methods) were being brought up to date with the latest developments and refinements in her work. It was March of 1993, and in spite of the warm strong sunshine at the beginning of the course, the weather had changed to snow with a bitterly cold wind.

Every day that I enjoy good health, I find myself wanting more than the usual amount of movement in my life, so when we had a little free time at the end of the day, I put on my warm clothes, and ventured out for a walk. After stretching my legs through the forest, I could not resist stopping for just a minute or two to talk to one of the trees growing quite close to this hotel.

I asked the tree how it felt about things, and it told me that some of the trees not far away were dying. I felt that they were starting to die early, so I asked the tree if there was anything that I personally could do to help, bearing in mind that I do not have 150 acres of land waiting to be planted up with trees. The tree showed me a picture of some daffodils. I could not see what the connection was between a clump of daffodils and trees. Then I saw some little blue flowers growing beside the daffodils, and I began to understand. Trees are just as sensitive to their environment as we are, and therefore in areas where mankind can influence their surroundings, we could plant beautiful flowers to make them happy.

A Talk with Jasper

On another day, Linda came over to the table where I was eating my lunch, and asked me if I would talk to Jasper, a chestnut horse who had been exceptionally difficult to work with.

Ten minutes later, she took me to his stall. There were angels standing around us who helped me to make contact with him. Linda asked if he wanted to stay with his present owner. I received a very clear "No". Was he still in his body? I looked and saw that there was a silver cord reaching upwards, and almost beyond the rafters, I saw his astral body floating around. Clearly he was several metres out of his body. I learnt from him that he did not want to re-enter his body, but wanted to disconnect with it altogether. Although he chose to incarnate, it was almost like an accident to end up in this particular body. He had not thought that it would be the way it was, and now he only wanted to get out of it.

Linda told me after I had finished channelling, that his particular body type and profile predisposed him to many personality problems, so that it was not easy for him to work with people. She also added that she had felt everything that I had told her about him, but wanted me to confirm it for her. I later spoke to Annegret Ast who had worked with the horse. She had also seen him floating around high up above his physical body. She was very aware that when he was in this state it was not possible for him to control his behaviour, and that that was why he was so dangerous to work with, so she determined that he should be kept in his stall, rather than risk anyone on the TTEAM course (Linda's course) getting hurt. The understanding sympathetic owner agreed to take him back home, where it was possible for him to run free in a field while she sorted out another solution for him. Annegret spoke with the horse to tell him that if he did not take the opportunities offered him by sympathetic people to work with him, and allow them to touch him, he would most probably find himself facing the same situation again in another body. Linda tried to talk to him in the night, but she said he was "out", and I did not manage to make contact with him again either.

Contact from a boxer dog..

One afternoon was spent working with dogs. Six dogs attended. Not all of them needed help, but as spectator, I found myself spellbound watching Linda work with a very hyperactive brown and white boxer. Physically it looked a healthy, and fit dog with a shiny coat, but mentally he was like a big bundle of uncontrollable over-reaction. He did not think, he just reacted, and did not appear to be very happy in spite of his kind owners. Although there was only a very small area in which to train him in the middle of the room, (this was after the weather had turned so wintry that we were grateful to be indoors, and not freezing in the riding school) Linda's methods proved very effective, and with the help of two assistants, the dog seemed to achieve quite a reasonable level of sanity and self-control by the end of the session.

In bed that night, as I closed my eyes with the intention of sleep, I caught a vivid rear view of this same boxer. The tense hind legs as he strained at his leash were unmistakable. He turned round and started to speak to me. He wanted to let us all know how grateful he was for the help he had received, and particularly to thank Linda. He said that he had never been able to experience himself in that way before. He had never been able to look at other dogs so thoughtfully. He had only understood reaction, not thinking, or just being. He was so grateful. Even if he was never able to experience those things again, something inside him had changed, a gift that he could hold forever.

Assisted Channelling

On the last day of the course we had a meeting all afternoon, and another one was planned before dinner. This only happened because some of TTEAM's most experienced practitioners were there, so this was an ideal time to discuss everything concerning the TTEAM teaching movement past, present, and future.

I have disliked meetings for as long as I can remember, especially if there is any disharmony, and even when things are going very smoothly. I feel that I get so stuck in my head, and my body craves physical movement and fresh air, and relief from the unwelcome mental effort and concentration. If it goes on for too long I get a head-ache, which can only be put right if I go and do something I enjoy more instead. I seldom get involved with the outcome of a debate, and my desire to leave the room becomes overwhelming. Therefore I explained to Linda that I wanted to go for a walk instead of attending the second meeting.

Linda asked me to do some channelling for TTEAM with the help of a tree while I was out. I agreed, but this posed a problem for me. There was quite a lot that she wanted to know, and if I carried out her instructions to the letter, I would have spent most of the available 'exercise time' stationary beside a tree with pad and pencil writing it all down while I froze in the cold winter air. The solution came to me while I was walking. I could feel the trees without touching them. Tree energy was in the air everywhere. Part of the atmosphere of the place was made up of the group consciousness of the forest. I appealed to this consciousness to aid my channelling. The result was that information flowed very easily. Just to doublecheck the accuracy of it, I paused for about two minutes in physical contact with one tree in particular, received further messages, and learnt that the previous channelling held good.

The content of the channelled information for TTEAM is not relevant to this book, whereas the way in which it came to me is. I learnt from this how the beings, trees in this case, in my environment are able to lend their power to help me access information. It explains why when I walk up into the mountains of Snowdonia in Wales, I experience a greater clarity of thought. Not only have I removed myself from the density of varied and often conflicting vibrations and thought forms to be found in the atmosphere of highly populated places, but the very rocks are giving out their energy. The Earth, where she is not covered with concrete, breathes out a certain vibrant energy that revives the human form, and can be tapped into for channelling, or for whatever it is most needed. This seems to be intensified if I radiate out love for the sources of the energies that I am enjoying. This opens up my aura, and makes it easier for me to receive. I thank the Earth, the trees, the rocks, the mountains, the streams, the rivers, the waterfalls, the lush vegetation with its lichens and mosses for the energy and beauty that they give out. The positive energies in most of this national park are not to be found everywhere. Other places where the Earth has been violated by mankind hold a sad ravaged energy, and seem to be badly in need of healing. Also ancient burial chambers are very suspect places. I will tell of my experiences with two of those later in this book.

Before closing this chapter, I would like to say a word about the nature of my animal communications. What I am currently capable of is so often misunderstood. Before now I have had people come to me and say, "Helena, we have a cat here, and we think that it is unhappy, so please will you ask it what is wrong?" For this kind of communication, it is usually necessary to use telepathy, where there is a direct mind to mind link between the channel and the animal. There are people who have developed this into a fine art, but I am not one of them. Most of my work so far has consisted of meeting animals and others in another dimension, and communication with the conscious mind of a living animal is not something I have learnt. In the case of Jasper, I feel that the information was relayed to me by the angels, who felt that Linda and Annegret should have their findings confirmed. (It also helped me to discover that my channelling agreed with the information that, unknown to me, they had already received.) With the boxer-dog, the dog came to me in an out-of-the-body state, so in neither case did I use telepathy directly from physical mind to physical mind with a living animal. There was no two-way conversation with the dog next door when I felt like it!

Chapter 5

Life Outside My Body, and Discerning My Discarnate Friends

With a chapter title like this one, it would not be surprising if a whole book were to follow, for books have already been written about such topics by others. Instead I intend to write something slightly shorter, and to write it based entirely upon my personal experiences. Looking back it seems amazing to me that even in the early 1980s I had already developed the habit of writing my experiences down in a selection of notebooks, in spite of having no intention of ever writing a book, or recounting them to anyone. It was simply part of my own research, but this has enabled me to retell the stories accurately.

I feel that everything that has been given to me has been given to me to share with others, and after a chapter about Jasper floating about above his body, it really seems a good moment to tackle this topic.

There are many different degrees of leaving the physical body. The most dramatic of these is commonly called "Death", where the soul leaves the physical body for good, and the silver cord (mentioned in the Bible) breaks, freeing the spirit to move towards the Light, although in the case of lost or Earth-bound souls it gets more complicated. I will write about them later.

A less permanent departure from the body can be managed by the astral body, which is much less dense than the physical. There is never any risk of getting lost out there, because we remain attached by the silver chord, which ensures our return trip, although getting back into the body smoothly is sometimes harder.

It is also possible that just the mental body goes out. This too is astral travel in a sense, and it is the type that I have had the most experience of, for it is very useful when accessing other realities.

I have noticed with great interest that when it comes to things that I don't really need to be able to do, I am given just enough of a taste of each type of experience to know that it is real, and then, by whatever the forces are that control my destiny, I am moved on to something else. This has been the case with astral travel.

My first memory of leaving my body this way was rather dramatic. When I described it to a trance medium, he said, "That sounds like going into full trance to me." It happened in the summer of 1982. I was going through a fairly emotionally insecure period of my life, which I feel made me rather less well attached to my body than usual. It was sometime after 2.00 a.m. when I woke up in bed, and immediately I became conscious (awake), I felt myself being sucked upwards leaving my body through my head. It was an involuntary movement. As I passed out of my body, to my horror, I saw somebody else sliding down into it. At the time, I did not know what the somebody was, whereas now I am sure that it was an extra-terrestrial being. It must have been coming down facing the wrong way, and turned itself round later, for there was a moment when we were face to face. The face looked very tense, and I did not like the feel of the vibrations which were strange to me. The person had no hair, and was a greenish-grey colour. The ears stuck out rather, and he(?) wore no clothes. He had a much squarer type of body than a human.

I floated up to the ceiling, and when I looked down, I saw my own body which had now been sat up on the bed with the E.T. inside it. Furthermore, I saw about twelve of his friends, all the same greenish-grey colour as him, sitting round my body in a large semicircle. (I could not actually tell what sex any of them were, so I am using the masculine for convenience.)

These beings were not of such a physical nature as humans, for I perceived a corner of the bedroom where there was no door, and yet this was their entry point. It was like some kind of astral passageway that led into the room. Although from my position on the ceiling it was not possible to tell what they were saying, I did gather that it was a question and answer session between the group, and the one in my body. My intuition tells me that they were probably trying to find out something about how it felt to be in a human body. I had no control. I was just an onlooker. When they had found out whatever they wanted to know, I spontaneously descended feet first, reentered my body, and the E.Ts. vanished. This was all so unexpected. I had had no idea that something like this could happen to me. I found it un-nerving to discover that I could be taken out of my body like that. Somewhat shaken, although I did not really need to, I made a trip to the bathroom just to make sure that I was back in my body, and that I and no-one else was in control of it. Having established that these things were so, at around 2.30 a.m., I climbed back into bed, and slept soundly until morning.

When I spoke to my friends about this, the advice that they gave me was that if I did not know with whom I was dealing, then it would be better not to permit it.

On 25th. August 1982 there were three or four (I lost count) more attempts by these beings to put me into full trance. They knew enough about me to realise that one of my childhood dreams had been to become a ballet dancer, so they promised me that if I would come with them, I would be rewarded by this dream of mine coming true. They would arrange it for me. For a split second I wavered, captivated by pictures of me looking ready to dance "Swan Lake." Then I realised how ridiculous it was that this could ever happen, (I was too old to start ballet seriously, lacking in athletic ability, and the wrong build to make a success of it.) More important to me than this, I decided that anyone who appealed to my vanity and my ego in this way in order to get something from me could hardly be coming from a place of light! During the first of these attempts I was at least one third of the way out, leaving through the head again, but with the sensation that someone was trying to pull me out of my body by my hair.

Before things went any further, I somehow managed to use such a force of my own will to go back in, that I found myself slipping back down into my physical body. I also used a mantra that someone had given me, although I have long since forgotten what it was, and by the third repetition I was back in my body lying peacefully awake in my bed. The following times, the E.Ts. were even less successful. It seemed that each time I consciously chose to resist with all of my energy, I grew stronger. I also cried for help to my guardian angels, and one of them became visible to me that night just before the last attempt to get me out of my body. I looked at the clock, and saw that it was 4.30 a.m..

I remember several occasions after that, when I was aware of other entities trying to coax me out of my body. The early hours of the morning were a favourite time. . They had no power over me. Resisting them helped to develop my spiritual strength. I had to let it be known that I was not available without my conscious consent for exploitation by forces who were not entirely "light" or known to me.

I found that I was going through one of many periods of testing. Another way in which I was troubled at nights, was by the visits of "Earth-bound souls", or entities from the astral realms who were still hanging on to the Earth plane, instead of leaving the physical reality, and making their way to the Light. Later in my life, I was to learn how to help these lost souls, but at this stage I was only concerned with persuading them to leave me in peace, and getting rid of them. I was afraid.

I had various experiences, most of them occurring in the early hours of the morning. The spirits would wake me up by making their presence so obvious that I could no longer sleep. Sometimes they would sit on top of me, so that I could not move. There was one man who looked just how I imagine an escaped convict to look; bald, strong, tough, and rough with a really hard face full of anger and aggression. He wanted to smash the mirror in my bedroom when he saw his reflection in it. He did not succeed, but I saw him try to put his fist through it, as though he did not like how his face looked, and wanted to destroy himself. Another time he had such a firm grasp on my right forearm, that again, I could not move. When he sat on me, it was almost impossible to breath, and his energy felt very oppressive. I was too afraid to even consider trying to talk to this fellow, so I dealt with it by mentally screaming for help from "God". At that stage in my life, I had little conscious contact with angels, or guardian angels, and still thought of God as some kind of almighty powerful being in the sky if he did exist. Whether he existed or not, I was desperate enough to give him a try, as I could think of nothing better. The man always left eventually, whether it was of his own will, or because I received outside help I could not always say, but after I had spoken of this with psychic friends about eighteen months after his visits started, he was permanently removed from my presence with the help of discarnate beings who were working for the Light.

With hindsight, I would say that this man was attracted to me because he found that I was sensitive enough for him to be able to make his presence known to me. These lost or Earthbound souls are often very frustrated when they discover that people still living in physical bodies cannot see them, hear them, or feel their touch. They are still trying to live their existence on the Earth-plane instead of moving away to another dimension where things are no more or less solid than they are.

Concerning calling for "God" when in trouble, I have noticed since then that "Beings of Light" will sometimes respond to such a call if the need is genuine, and their presence is appropriate. In the early 1980's a medium managed to find out for me that I had a special guide or protector at this time called Graham. Calling for Graham when in distress never failed.

One night I lay in bed in a blurry hard-to-define state of awareness struggling with some kind of alien forces. My body was being "shared", and I could not dislodge the other occupant. I called for Graham who did not appear immediately, so I raised the pitch of my voice hoping he would hear me better. Graham arrived at high speed, and the aliens left instantly. "...but your voice did sound funny!" he said. He gave me the picture of the two of us in a dry sunny desert with just a few rocks, boulders, and scrub-like vegetation, which felt so down-to-earth that I found it easy to relax again, for I had been taken out of the darkness of my bedroom. Graham was wearing light brownish-green coloured clothes, and looked a very normal human being. I assumed that he had looked like that in one of his past lives, and that he found it a suitable identity for the occasion. This was the only time that I ever saw him. When the vision faded, I found myself lying there alone in bed very wide awake.

Having made this conscious contact with Graham who was clearly one of the "good guys", things began to get better. I was understandably still very nervous, and not ready to trust that my night time visitors had my best welfare as their priority.

In November of 1982 I awoke from a deep sleep at 5.45 a.m. with the feeling that I had been woken. I climbed out of bed and walked around a bit, noticing how sore my back felt, as I was still recovering from a visit to the osteopath after a back injury. I got back into bed, and fell into a light sleep. Again I awoke feeling that I had been woken by something, and aware of the presence of several beings around my bed very close to me, who seemed to be trying to lift me horizontally as I lay there on my back. I felt my body being twisted around, almost a sensation of swaying to and fro. As I called for, and implored Graham to come and take them all away, I felt someone holding my left hand. Eventually they all left. I calculated that there must have been at least three of them. To my surprise afterwards, I found that my back-ache had eased very considerably. In fact at that point, I felt no pain at all. This was a clue to me that the energies around me were good now, and that I had clearly received some healing to my back while they were there, even though I had asked them to leave.

During the early hours of 20th. December the same year, while half awake, and half asleep, I became aware of a spirit presence which seemed to be coming and going. Then very clearly I saw a spirit child at the side of my bed offering me peanuts. Still suspicious, I declined, but my efforts to try and talk to her with my physical voice brought me into a fully awake state. I lost sight of her, but realising that she was a spirit child, I began to wish that I had accepted her little offering. She was so sweet. She had brown eyes, and long mousey-coloured hair down her back.

After a brief interval, during which I remained awake, I felt a spirit presence much closer. I alerted Graham, but calmly this time, as I dared to believe that it was probably a friendly spirit. I felt someone clasping my right hand with both of theirs, and another hand on my left hand. The usual tingling sensation that I associated with these occasions was present in my body. I drifted away, leaving the earthly reality, and found myself walking about somewhere else. Although there seemed to be some slight law of gravity, I needed no effort to go up or down stairs. My body felt very light-weight, I had the power to reason, and knew that my physical body was lying motionless in my bed. This other body that I was now experiencing wore no clothes, which strangely did not worry me in the least, as it seemed so normal. However, I did not meet anyone! I also noticed as I looked down at my body, that my skin appeared to be equally white all over, whereas had I been in my physical body, my extremities would most probably have looked rather purple by comparison, as my circulation is not particularly efficient. After this experience I slept very soundly.

My next lesson in life outside the physical body took place in the early hours of 5th. January, 1983. I had been sleeping rather lightly, and woke up enough to be aware of the familiar tingling feeling all over my body. The vibrations of the spirit presence around me felt friendly, so deciding that it could be the "good guys" again, I chose to let happen whatever was about to happen, but took the precaution of muttering Graham's name a few times just in case I was wrong.

I found myself walking around in a small room with a red tiled floor, and started to run round it, as I was aware of feeling slightly chilly. I moved on to somewhere else in dimly lit conditions, which continued throughout this experience. I knew that I had left my body lying in bed, because of the tingly feeling that I had had before I left it. Meanwhile I thoroughly enjoyed exploring my environment to find out which things I could put my hands and arms straight through, and which things were solid enough to make a proper contact with. It was as though I was aware of two different dimensions at once, and that as both were equally visible to me, the only way of knowing what belonged to what was to touch everything and find out which things were of the same density as my astral body, and which things I could pass straight through.

This time I was taken back to my bedroom by being put on a bed of the same density as my astral body. I was upset about this, because I was having such a good time that I wanted to continue wandering about looking at things. A lady who must have been one of my guides, seeing that I was about to leave the bed explained kindly but firmly that I must stay on it, that it had to be. I protested, but still on the bed, an instant later recovered normal consciousness in my physical body wide awake on my own bed. My guides had brought me safely back. The strange thing about this story is that throughout my conversation to the lady guide, she spoke to me in French, and I always replied to her in German. I almost feel that I was passing through a sort of dream state as I returned to my body.

Over two years passed without my guides giving me any more lessons in astral travel. Then in October of 1985, it started again. Two of these experiences are worthy of mention.

The first of these was in some respects very like dreaming, and yet I was much more conscious than one usually is in a dream, and very aware that I was outside my body. I had a journey to make, and chose to go on foot through the woods, as making contact with nature seemed much more important than taking a shorter route. I was running through the trees, and realised that time did not matter. I felt that this journey was not really necessary, but sensing a pleasure in living and being, I chose to carry on running at an easy pace. In spite of this, I started wondering if I was going too fast for my fitness level, but observed that although I had covered a considerable distance, I had not even begun to tire, and each step was as springy and effortless as the last. As I was fully aware that my physical body was lying asleep or unconscious on the bed, I noted how in my astral body, I had no need to breath to keep it going, not even when I was running.

The second experience was two months later, when I had another incident in the night, only this one had none of the dreamlike quality of the first.

At about 4.00 a.m. I awoke to find myself at the start of another experience. I was lying in bed inside my physical body, when I sensed something like pressure fairly evenly distributed over the whole of me. I thought about resisting or sending it away, but in the absence of fear, and feeling more inclined to go back to sleep than make any effort, I lay passively there waiting to see what would happen next. I found myself in a very sleepy state sitting on a small round soft grey stool very close to my body. I felt completely droopy, and was not making any effort either mental or physical. At the same time I could still relate to the body lying in the bed, which was very relaxed, and thought that maybe I should take it to the bathroom. I heard a voice close to my right ear and slightly behind me say "I think we had better lie you down again." Following this, I became aware of some force or forces outside myself lowering my top half very slowly and gently back into my body. I was not aware of my legs moving. I think that they must have been very close to my physical ones already. I was so intent on carrying out my decision to go to the bathroom with my physical body, that I tried to turn my bedside light on before my two bodies were properly lined up. This meant that although at least one of my bodies had a hand round the light switch, I was unable to operate my fingers to move it. I have to guess a little bit at cause and effect here. It could be that the astral hand reached the light switch before the physical one did, or even the other way round, but they definitely did not arrive on the light switch together. My clue that the two bodies were not yet properly aligned came from a heaviness in my head. I could not move it at all. It was not ready to follow the rest of my body as I tried to reach the light. As my unseen helpers finished putting me back into place, my co-ordination gradually returned, and I was able to turn on the light successfully.

Later in the day, I tried to work out what lesson I was to learn from these things. My conclusions were as follows. Although I submitted to it, I did not leave my body through my own energy. Several other entities were looking after me. These individuals were caring, as evidenced by the gentleness with which I was laid back into my physical body on the bed. I noted that I was not kept out of my body against my will, but escorted back in, even if I had tried to move too soon. I was in such a drowsy state of consciousness when I was sitting up on the stool, that I had the feeling that my guides were thinking, "I don't think we can do more than this with her tonight."

It was in this fashion that I learnt to be selective about who I was working with, and it is my hope that any developing psychics who read this chapter will find it interesting and helpful, and take comfort from it.

Chapter 6

The Story of the Elephant Servants

I do hesitate to put this in, as although I regard it as excellent material myself, part of me is feeling that it all sounds too far fetched to be credible to others. Then I remember that this could be especially helpful to those recalling their own extra-terrestrial lives, and that if some of those reading it cannot quite swallow it whole, at least it is full of philosophy and teaching that can only be valuable.

In addition, the story moves me, and therefore may move and touch the hearts of others, so here I am sharing it.

I recalled this lifetime during one of my Light Institute sessions in Mexico during the summer of 1993. (I refer to "The Light Institute of Galisteo" founded in New Mexico, U.S.A. by Chris Griscom.) My facilitator helped me through this session.

"I find myself on another planet, and look at myself with interest to see what kind of being I am. My head, which is roughly round, has two little white things stuck out on either side near the top. It is connected to my body by a thin black piece, or it may be a very dark blue like my body which is very vaguely cubic. I have two legs like black sticks with a knob on the end of each. My three pairs of fully retractable arms can be withdrawn into the body, and stuck out again when needed. I look like a computer or a robot. Very strange! As eyes I have big slits that can open and close. My rather cubic bottom part is almost like a separate section from my slightly cubic top part. There are others like me here, and we appear to be full of electricity with computer-like brains. The doctors on this planet sometimes find themselves doing brain surgery on the rest of the population when bits are wearing out, and need renewing.

When I look around at the landscape, I see dark rocks and hard roadways. Evidently we are quite mechanised, for we have transport that can travel both on the land, and also, propelled by jet-like engines that give out blue exhaust, through the atmosphere (whatever that may consist of). The engines are at the back, and flying uses more fuel than travel on the land. We pick things up using magnetism, which is why we neither have nor need any fingers. In their place we just have knobs. With three sets of arms it is possible to perform quite complicated tasks, the brain being capable of operating all six arms independently at the same time.

Our houses are built in the rocks, which makes them a little like fortresses, for we are very warlike, and from the portals of our house I see something that looks rather like a cannon gun. It is used for defence against other galactics, and also for battles between ourselves. There is a darkened place on the planet where there has been a recent battle.

There is a spaceship arriving from another planet. When it lands, it is supported by legs with feet, and then a door is opened which makes a ramp sloping down to the ground. The whole ship is totally different from ours. The galactics stepping out of it look more like humans than we do, but their heads have flat tops and advanced brains, and they are equipped with many more senses than humans. Their colour is rather white, but it has light green tinges here and there. We are afraid that they will colonise our planet, so we kill them with our very powerful weapons that produce blasts of blue light and flying black stones with lethal gases.

Now my attention is drawn to some other creatures that the foreigners have brought with them. These beings look like animals. In fact they look exactly like elephants, except that they have the same light colouring as the people. They are their servants. A number of these "Elephant Servants" walk down the

41

ramp onto our planet, and we decide to capture them and use them for ourselves. We put them into small square pens with six or seven of them crowded together so that they can barely move. This experiment of using them to serve us rarely works, because the Elephant Servants are used to responding to telepathic messages from their masters, and not to our electrical commands. Many of them perish, and another problem is that they carry more light than we do. (We do not really carry any noticeable light.) The light is a problem because we do not know how to deal with it. Nonetheless, we are very frustrated with our inability to use them. I can see myself banging my head on the rocks in frustration and anger because the servants do not work for us.

The Elephant Servants are full of wisdom and humility, and have at least seven major strongly developed senses, and there is visible light shining out of them. One of the larger ones who looks like a big bull elephant is saying, "This is not our planet. We do not belong here. Let us go home." We are so angry that we blow them all up. We do not like it when we cannot have what we want, when we are not obeyed.

Their presence was starting to stir feelings of love and compassion, which is not normal for our people. Therefore we were very afraid of these feelings, which we felt would have caused chaos in our society, and that is another reason why we blew the elephants up. They were seen as a threat by us. Before they came, we felt nothing. Since they touched us with their light, those of us who were physically near to them now feel pain, and do not know how to kill the pain.

The pain is severe, and regarded as a physical disorder that might impair our work capacity, and consequently regarded as a hazard to our society and organisation. It is this possibility of the resulting malfunction, and not out of compassionate grounds, that one of our technician doctors spends a long time checking out my electrical system in the hopes of removing this "pain", but there is nothing that he can do. Sometimes we do malfunction because of it.

We have no heart energy or heart organ in our bodies. We are not equipped to carry the higher emotions, which is why it is so painful for us when these vibrations are inflicted on us from the light of the Elephant Servants.

There are other less spiritually orientated visitors from space who come with a lot of red energy, and who, although they do not look at all like us, are much closer to us with their vibrational frequency. As their planet is physical like ours, they are able to bring special types of rocks and minerals, and we are trying to trade with them. We sometimes travel to their planet, which I see as very red, in ships. They have sex which we do not, but it is a rough primitive civilisation in which they have little respect for each other. They are quite varied in temperament, whereas our people are close to identical. We build new ones (people) ourselves. We take the necessary materials, and make them like robots. It is very complicated. We use a special technical procedure that puts the life into them which we carry out in a laboratory. There is a moment when there is a flash of light, and this is when the soul energy enters the new body. In order to achieve this, we have to go to a being like a very tall angel who organises the souls waiting for incarnation on our planet. We do not like it very much, because this angel comes from the light, and we are not really light beings.

In our society we are more or less equal, but sometimes we fight between ourselves concerning who is going to do what. Sometimes this ends in death, but not always, as in minor squabbles, we just knock each other about, whilst in major battles there are usually deaths. When the physical vehicle is destroyed, there is death in the sense that that particular incarnation is terminated in that form, but some of us do not leave the planet immediately, especially when there are feelings of revenge. This gives those of us left here a hard time, as not only do we have to put up with hearing something that resembles jeering laughter coming from them, but they also cause trouble with the mechanism of the blue parts of our bodies, which then seem to go wrong or short circuit. We sleep as humans do, sometimes for long hours, and these spirits will come and torment us in our dreams. How badly depends on our relationship to each particular soul when it was in a body incarnated with us. They do not take revenge haphazardly. Sometimes they come in groups, small groups fortunately, up to six or seven of them together, but in any quantity they are damaging to our equipment and to us."

At this point in my session, I seem to have made a leap to the other side of my death, so I cannot say how I died, although if I had to guess, I would suggest mechanical breakdown, or electrical failure, or these two combined with death on the battle field, but the exact details of it are not important for this story. In spite of this leap forward through time, I was still able to look back and see more of the background to this life.

(I must point out here that this is the only time when working with a facilitator that I was not guided to recall my death, as this is an important part of the therapy. It was most probably because of the spontaneous leap to the other side of that death that we forgot to go back to it. The story line was exciting!)

We were someone else's experiment. They were technically a very advanced race who chose to create thinking robots who could work for them, but their plan went wrong because we developed our own sense of identity, and did not care what we did. We were to have been used for building spaceships and even roads, but we wanted the power for ourselves. So the beings who started our civilisation abandoned us to our own chaos. We did not care. It meant more freedom.

We did not have any family connections or friends. (No sex, so no relatives.) Sometimes we fought each other. Sometimes we did not. We were free from any (loving) emotional ties with our fellow beings. Naturally this was rather a dark and unenlightened type of existence, so normally people only allowed a small part of themselves to incarnate into this kind of body, the greater part remaining in the light at least until the incarnation here was complete, as this was considered "safer".

In my case only a small part of my consciousness had entered into my body. I felt no pain as I entered, just numb. Most of the emotions were absent in us, but hatred and anger and certain other negative ones were still possible. It was part of the education of my soul to experience life on that level, to experience life where love was absent.

I spent a long time between lives, as I needed so much healing. It had been a life without a heart literally, and only after joining the angels did I begin to grow a heart again, and eventually something like an astral body of a human. The angels told me that not all souls manage to survive a life living in that darkness, but that I have been saved through the magnetic effect of the light of the Elephant Servants, which helped to draw me back towards the light, something I could never forget.

Many thousands of years on when I was ready to incarnate again, I went not to the planet of the Elephant Servants, but to work with the elephants on planet Earth in India, for I knew that I owed them a great debt, and I lived two lives as an elephant boy there. I had made a vow in between lives that I would one day return the service to them, but first I needed these lives working with them to strengthen the connection. Now in this lifetime I seek to help the animal kingdom through the writing of my books.

It is important that before the end of my session, I chose to release this karmic contract, as it is better to serve from a position of unconditional love, rather than through obligation from previous vows.

In the days following this session, the picture that stayed in my mind the most clearly was the first view I had had of the Elephant Servants as they walked down the ramp of that visiting spaceship, so majestic, so magnificent, such a picture of wisdom and love and dedication. Just watching them in a state of wonder had really moved me.

The message that I received from my Higher Self at the end of the session was that this was a very big lesson in the power of the light, for the light from the Elephant Servants had penetrated my darkness even when I had no heart.

Chapter 7

Seven Angel Stories

I do not know everything about angels, but in these changing times at the dawning of the Age of Aquarius, many more angels are coming close to us than before. It seems to be so that they can help with the raising of the level of human consciousness. My personal inner awareness tells me that it is the whole of creation that is changing, not just people. Therefore I wish to start my angel stories with a tale of how I experienced an angel influencing an animal.

1. Angelic Help With a Horse

It was about two years ago when I was schooling a thoroughbred horse for a client. The horse, Dick (not his real name), had a reputation for being an unpredictable nut-case, but I had known him for some time, and knew that he usually settled down quite well during the work that I did with him in the field. It was a cold windy day, which tends to put highly strung horses rather on their toes, but Dick remained calm and obedient. He had recently had a cold, and been off work with it, but now he was thought to have fully recovered, so I was asked to ride him. The movement, however, caused some catarrh to enter his nasal cavities, so he blew his nose determinedly to try and get rid of it. Stringy lumps of it dangled in the most revolting way from his nostrils, so in a further attempt to rid himself of this irritating substance, he proceeded to toss his head violently. Aided by the wind as well, it flew out and upwards, and then back at him, hitting him in the face. This was too much for Dick, who reacted as though some strange and terrifying outside force, that had to be escaped from as soon as possible, was attacking him. He fled!

The faster he galloped, the more he frightened himself, and the more convinced he became that he had to keep on fleeing no matter what. I tried everything that I knew in my endeavours to reach him, calm him down, and have him understand that it was actually safe to stop. Sometimes he would slacken his pace very slightly, and begin to raise my hopes, but then without any form of stimulus, he would set off again at full gallop. Had this taken place on open ground where there was space for his antics, it would not have mattered. It would have been quite safe, for it is not difficult to sit on a galloping horse. I would have been very happy to enjoy the speed, and wait for him to stop when he was ready. As it was, we were in a field which was too small to take the inevitable corners at that pace safely. His body was taut with tension, and he leaned in like a motorbike as he turned. Balance did not come into it, and any moment I was expecting him to fall flat on his side, as his feet slipped from under him on the wet slippery muddy ground.

A further worry was what could happen if I was unable to turn him. There were fences with barbed wire, dykes, trees, and treacherous boggy uneven ground. A brilliant horse with its mind on the job could have taken a clean safe leap out of the field at a carefully selected spot, even when travelling at that pace, but this horse was mindless. Dick's panic level was far too high for him to be capable of calculating anything. He was a danger to both of us. He could break his own neck and mine if he galloped blindly into one of these obstacles. He listened to nothing. "He is not even my own horse! I am responsible for his welfare. Somehow I have to save him for his owner, and look after myself as well so that I can go as planned to Germany in two days time," I thought to myself, "but my repertoire of stopping methods is totally exhausted!"

I had tried amongst many other things to use the calming vibrations of my voice to relax him to no avail, but out of desperation, in spite of my belief in self-help, and said in a voice of such amazing calmness that even I was surprised to hear it, I prayed out loud. "Dear Lord, please calm this horse for me!" Dick was travelling full tilt at the time, and had just made the turn towards the stables. Therefore he was more determined to keep going than ever, but the effect was immediate. Every muscle in his body seemed to relax at the same time, as he quietly came back to a walk. Although in a shaken state myself, I was then able to carry on working him in all paces just as though nothing had happened. He remained perfectly relaxed and obedient for the rest of the morning.

I was absolutely certain that I had had outside help. I had been in a situation where I could not help myself, so I had asked for help, and an angel who must have been very nearly sitting on my shoulder ready to rescue me, but not wanting to intervene unasked, had done what I could not do, and calmed the horse for me, so that once again he became safe to ride. The help had been instant. The change in the horse dramatic. I would never have believed that any animal or person could change for the better so suddenly, had I not been there to experience it.

I gave many thanks to the angel.

I do not believe that the Lord, or God is a person sitting on a golden throne surrounded by angels somewhere up in the clouds, but this experience was proof enough to me that anyone praying to whatever name goes with their own belief-system as the highest source of good or light, be it Allah, The Great White Spirit, Jesus, or whoever, will be heard either by an angel, or some other being in the service of the Light, and may receive help if it is appropriate. (I mean where the need is real.)

2. A Guardian Angel in the Woods
My second story took place on 6th. February 1994. On this day I was indulging myself with an all-day walk in the beautiful hills of Snowdonia. It was almost inevitable that the last few miles would be walked in the dark at that time of the year, but instead of choosing an easy route which would finish along the smooth even surface of a metalled road as I usually did, I could not resist the woodland path. The sky was clouded over rendering the night very dark, and what light there might have been seemed to be kept out by the trees. I was walking along the side of a steep hill along a very narrow path, so whereas the ground sloped steeply

upwards on my right, to the left it fell away like the edge of a precipice. There were many tree roots and small boulders to trip over, alternating with slippery patches of mud. I was carrying a very small map-reading torch, which I not only used to spot the afore-mentioned hazards, but also tried to remember to point it upwards often enough to avoid losing an eye on one of the twigs from the frequent low tree branches which were completely invisible without a torch. In spite of the outstanding day-time beauty of this place, I was beginning to get doubts about the wisdom of choosing such a perilous path to negotiate in the darkness of night. "It would be a shame if I fell and strained or broke my ankle up here in the dark when I am so nearly back at the car park, especially after all of the successful miles I have already walked today," I thought to myself. Even the usual sheep seemed to be absent just then, and I considered myself to be totally alone.

Imagine my surprise when immediately following those thoughts, I saw and heard someone walking very close beside me. I knew instantly that this person was not of the same dimension, and felt no fear, but a pleasant feeling of companionship. The man wore a full length light beige raincoat, a dark brown hat, and mid-brown trousers. He walked very slightly behind me and to my left, but so close that his body almost merged with mine. I could see all of this without turning my head, including his handsome face, and heard his brisk steps as his feet met the crisp leaves on the ground. "I am being cared for," I said silently to myself. "Even if I did fall over something, I suppose that it would all work out all right with him there," I continued. "I think that we can manage without trying that," he said. "O.K. then let's give that experiment a miss," I agreed, thinking how much nicer it would be if I did remain on my feet. I told him that I would appreciate it if he would stay by me all the way to the car, and gathered telepathically that that was what he was intending to do.

I relaxed, and enjoyed the remainder of my walk enormously.

I have no idea if this man had ever walked with me before, if he is always with me, or if he is only "on duty" when I go for these long hikes; but I marvelled over the knowledge that it is not just when

I am doing so called 'important work' that someone looks after me, but all the time. I had not even the faintest suspicion that someone was walking with me, but I feel now that he had been there all day with me, although he only revealed his presence to me to comfort me when he heard my thoughts about damaging myself. Before that, it was not necessary that I should know that he was there, especially as I was enjoying being alone! Even then, the sound of his footsteps, and my awareness of his body and clothes only lasted long enough for me to have a good look at him, and after that it was just a telepathic communication.

That was my second angel story. It brought the comment from a friend, "He was an angel, but he did not look like an angel!?" Personally I do not have any difficulty with the concept that any being who is fulfilling the role of guardian angel is capable of assuming whatever appearance fits the situation on the day. A change of clothes is just a change of thoughts. How simple! It is also possible that some of these guardian angels are actually beings who have agreed to help and guide us through our lives (when we are listening), and that they are not strictly speaking angels, but discarnate beings who are more evolved than the individual who is being helped. These are my thoughts about it. They could be right. They could be wrong. The only thing that really matters to me is not getting the correct definitions or terminology, but knowing that help is there, and will always be there, even if I cannot see it. This last point leads me into my third angel story, which took place on 3rd. August, 1993 when I was meditating with my friend Margot.

3. Angel Teachings, Mostly About Trust

I found myself standing on the peaceful shore of a horseshoe shaped bay. It was very sheltered with high rocks all round it. The sun shone, and the still blue water glistened in its light. I felt so secure and content there, that I felt I would never want to leave it.

In the middle of the water was what appeared to be a very small sailing ship with a single white sail. Beyond that I looked across to the rather narrow opening of the bay, and thought that to be on the water in such a small vessel in the bay would be alarming enough, as one did not know from the shore what treacherous currents lay concealed beneath the flat surface of the water, or how they could drag one out to sea, and how once through the opening of the bay and in the open water how vulnerable one would be to the ocean tides and currents. While contemplating these horrors, I found myself sitting in the boat, which on closer inspection turned out to be less than a boat. It was just a raft with a sail. It was made from logs lashed together with fine rope, which all added to my sense of insecurity when away from the shore. The raft was taking me towards the opening in the rocks leading to the vast expanse of the open ocean. I looked at the opening, and saw that there was a shaft of light shining down onto the water there. When I followed the light upwards, it led to the angel realms, and I felt that they guarded the bay. As my raft began to gain momentum, I noticed that something like a piece of string was attached to the front of it, and seemed to be guiding the little vessel. When my gaze followed the string leading away from it, and I saw that the other end was held by the hand of an angel, it took away my fear of the sea.

As we travelled on across the open water, I noticed that I had an apple with me. I did not know how I came to have it. The raft took me to various foreign lands, and as I travelled I observed that I was touching new things, and feeling how they were, like testing or sampling the environment for interest, and to learn. At one port of call I found myself in a warm climate, where the local people, who were somewhat darker skinned than I was, lived in small round huts made of reeds or grasses. I seemed to be going about from one to another teaching, or helping in some way. I then became anxious concerning the whereabouts of the angel, and followed the now familiar string that connected the two of us in order to catch up with it. It seemed that the angel was always a step or two ahead of me just around the corner out of my view. As I managed to catch sight of the angel again and drew closer, it turned around and held up a hand to forbid me to come nearer. I understood that if I always had the angel close and in sight, I would become too preoccupied with its presence, and stop concentrating on my work, which I gathered was very important.

I knew this to be true, and that I must stop thinking about the angel, and just trust that its presence did not depend on my looking at it, and that it would always be there preparing my pathway, and looking after me when necessary.

I saw that I was giving the people many fruits. They looked like different kinds of apples. I was curious about this, and asked, "How did I come to have all this fruit to give away?" I was shown myself sitting on the raft crossing the ocean again, and saw that apples in great numbers were being showered down from the Heavens to me. I remembered the saying, 'To whom much is given, much is expected.'

The above meditation I regard as one of the apples, for I have noticed with increasing frequency that the experiences given to me in meditation are full of teaching, and these teachings can be passed on to others by the means of my writing.

Just for your interest, the angels seen in this story did look like angels!

As far as I know, in all of the journeys that I have made outside of my body, there has been an angel presence to guide and look after me. Sometimes there has also been a human presence (incarnate) as well to ensure that I make a safe return. Although I feel very happy and at home on these trips without a physical body, it makes a lot of sense to me to be escorted. It would be the same if I went to explore either Antarctica or the African jungle in the flesh, I would need someone well acquainted with the area, a local expert, to keep me safe and on a suitable path in this unknown terrain lest I not live to tell the tale. When meditating, an angel, an emissary of the Light, is the appropriate person. There always is one just for the asking if one needs it.

4. Two Different Kinds of Angels

On the 10th. June, 1988, I led myself in a meditation using questions suggested in the book "A Call to the Lightworkers" by Rhea Powers. It was simple to do. I first recorded the questions to ask myself or "lead me" onto a tape leaving a little gap between each, and then after putting myself into a suitable state with some relaxation exercises, I played the tape back to myself using the pause button to allow myself the necessary time to get the answers. It was a wonderful and informative meditation, but only the "angel bit" is relevant to this chapter, and a full account of how to do this exercise is to be found in the above-mentioned book.

In the meditation, it was planned to make a trip to whatever place or state was considered to be home before my first incarnation on Planet Earth. To facilitate this, I called for a teacher from "Home" to come and show me the way. First of all, I saw what I considered to be my usual angel, but then another one appeared who looked different. The first angel was a beautiful being surrounded in white light, and full of loving kindness. The second one had golden hair, white clothes, an even more transparent kind of energy body, and everything about it shone. I felt that it had great strength. It was this second angel who was to be my escort and teacher.

After we had travelled a little way, I noticed that we were standing in something like an energy current which was passing straight through us. This meant that both my body, and the body of my teacher (angel) rippled like reflections seen on water.

The rest of this meditation, which was very interesting to me, I am saving for a later chapter where it will be more relevant, as it does not give any more information about angels.

The following evening I participated in a meditation beautifully led by George Pratt, an inspired expert on the principles of meditation, and referred to in my first book. We were asked to ascend a staircase leading from the darkness into the light, and to visualise that we shed a garment on every step of the way. Each garment represented a different facet of our personality, the bits that we so often identify with that are not actually us, things that need to be left behind when walking in high places. I noticed on my way up that shedding my wrist watch seemed to have a particular significance.

On reaching the top of the staircase, where George left us free to experience whatever would come, I was met by the second angel of the previous evening, the one who had accompanied me home. This being seemed to be fulfilling the roles of guide and teacher for me, and took me to a beautiful place on a very light vibration, I mean much less dense that those of the Earth. I was equipped with a suitable body for that environment. With the angel close beside me, I was allowed to wander freely in a landscape where I found that I could pass through anything that I could see without causing any harm to my surroundings or myself. I moved in the ground, on it, or above it, and happily passed my hand through the trunk of a tree. The surrounding atmosphere was like a flowing energy which rippled through us.

I studied the appearance of my angel-guide with great interest. Having just moved through everything else I could see, it occurred to me that the best way to seek further knowledge of this being was very simply to move in and feel it from the inside rather than just look from the outside. Permission for this was granted, so I took up my temporary residence inside the angel. (Bear in mind that I had discarded my less desirable parts on the stairs when I took my clothes off, so the angel only had my better half to deal with!)

I learnt that he/she/it worked mainly with energy and energy currents, and that it could lay down strong lines or currents of this positive golden energy wherever they were needed in the atmosphere, and seemed to be currently engaged in bringing a strong band of it towards the Earth. The vibrations of this being felt pure and very powerful, and I was fascinated by the difference between the vibrations of this being, and my own. I sensed with absolute certainty that this angel had never experienced an incarnation on Earth, or anywhere else even the tiniest bit like it. I, on the other hand, have had many incarnations on Earth and other Planets, and particularly my experiences on the Earth, I felt, had really changed my aura/energy field. Instead of the very clear strong gold light, I saw that my aura was white with a peculiar soft quality about it which felt good. It was slightly opaque, a little bit like a thin white mist or cloud. The softness was the direct result of my experiences on Earth. In order to see myself properly and make these comparisons, it had been necessary to drift out of the angel's energy field, stand back a bit, and look at us both separately.

George was now asking his meditation group to come back again, so I thanked my guide, and very reluctantly thought about descending the staircase back into the darkness at the bottom. George did not put it like that, but I could not forget how dark it was there by comparison. This was so distasteful to me, that one of my spirit guides told me of another way. Following these instructions, I pictured my physical body fully clothed in the chair where I had left it holding out warm welcoming arms to me. I allowed my spirit body which I kept well away from the staircase to float down into my own loving arms. Even so, it was really hard to be properly 'back' for quite some time afterwards.

The evidence from these two meditations shows that not all angels have the same sort of energy field, and that some of them are very different from us. It all depends on whether or not that angel-soul has experienced life on Earth in my opinion. I am amongst those who believe that angels can incarnate on the Earth, just as another soul might 'graduate' to an angel state, and perhaps then back to a physical incarnation. When I meet an angel, if the energy field is revealed to me, it is possible to see whether or not this has happened. I can only see the things that I am shown, and I am not always shown everything. I think that it is not always the best use of energy for me to be shown all that is there, for some information may not be relevant for the occasion. I am sure that knowledge is given to me when it is needed, and when I am ready to understand it.

5. Help From the Elohim Angels

This event happened when I was participating in one of Linda Tellington-Jones's week-long TTEAM workshops in December of 1988, and the story begins in a pub in Kaltenkirchen, north of Hamburg, Germany, while we were having lunch together. Without realising what I was doing, I spontaneously opened up my auric field when confiding something close to my heart with my neighbour. This made me very vulnerable to any near-by energies, and suddenly I felt something awful in my solar plexus. My appetite for the salad that I was eating deserted me instantly. I felt nervous, and very ill at ease, and my hands started to shake as I tried to finish the food for which I was not hungry. I wondered at how easily I had become upset. For the remainder of that day I was unusually nervous and lacking in confidence, and found it very hard to ride the horses properly due to my inexplicable fear which made me want to clutch at the reins the whole time. Luckily the shaking and loss of appetite had subsided.

The following morning my nerves were awful, and I seemed to be holding a surfeit of nervous energy in my solar plexus. Carrying this was exhausting. By 10.00 a.m., exasperated, I excused myself from Linda's workshop, explaining that I was in need of some quiet time by myself before I could carry on. I knew that in that state I was next to useless with the horses, and felt that I was wasting both my own and everyone else's time if I continued without first doing something about it.

In my room, although I had not any music to assist me, I did a Kundalini meditation consisting of wild chaotic movement in an attempt to rid myself of some of my excess tension. Then I lay down on my bed and tuned in. I became aware that I needed a 'clearing'. It seemed that while we were having lunch in that pub, I had picked up the energy of a discarnate man dressed in black, and I was currently suffering from his feelings of fear and discomfort. He had been able to penetrate my auric field and had attached himself to my solar plexus, because I was so open at that moment, and had not surrounded myself in light or taken any other measure to protect myself. Having first called the Elohim angels to help me, I spoke to him explaining how inappropriate it was for him to be there, that he no longer had a physical body of his own, and that it was ruining my life having him around. Furthermore, I told him that he had been there plenty long enough to benefit from contact with me and my philosophy, and that he would only experience real happiness if he left. I informed him that I was making arrangements for him to do this easily with help from the angels and a shaft of white light for him to use as a bridge from this dimension into the light where he belonged and would be looked after, and that there was nothing to fear.

I had had 'clearings' before with the help of a human therapist, this variety of clearing being the removal of (unwanted by me) astral entities or lost souls (also referred to in chapter five) residing in my aura or physical body. Now I was alone, so I would have to clear myself with the help of the angels. Rhea Powers had trained me to visualise the shaft of light which effectively creates one, and at the same time I saw a number of angels forming a circle around it. Next I felt two discarnate hands reach into my solar plexus and pluck something out of it. They were removing the energy of the man in black. The Elohim angels were really present. I had not expected that they would make it so easy for me. Immediately I began to sigh with relief, as I lay peacefully on my bed in a beautifully relaxed state feeling totally comfortable and myself again. After a moment or two of just lying there and enjoying this, I left the bed, and took a shower. Water is a great cleanser, not only of the body, but also of the aura. Completely refreshed, I rejoined Linda's workshop.

6. Archangels
My sixth angel story is a much more recent event in my life, and it concerns archangels. The story part is very short, so I will tell that first.

Towards the end of 1994 I was feeling very frustrated with the way in which my life was going. It had been well organised, but little by little things seemed to have got out of hand, and therefore I felt that I was achieving very little whilst running in all directions to manage this. Well, wouldn't you feel frustrated? There was no easy answer to put it right, so as I lay in bed, I called to the angels for help. "If I am supposed to be doing better than this, then I need help before I can manage it. Help!" I felt annoyed that things were not going how I thought they should. In front of me I saw six or seven angels. I did not quite manage to count them up, but they looked like a committee to me, and they appeared to be considering my case. I fell asleep.

In the days that followed, nothing actually changed, but I felt a distinct shift in the energies around me which made it much easier for me to come to terms with life as it was. I felt calmed.

An exceptionally kind friend called Gila Galitzine invited me to join her workshop called "Reise in die Zukunft" or "Journey into the Future". So off to Germany I went. Gila led this quite beautifully with the wonderful support of her husband Michael who organised lovely music for us. She had always had close connections with the angels, and the very first evening she told me how there were seven archangels. Suddenly I knew that that was exactly what I had seen, even though the last thing that I had expected was for my prayers to be answered by seven archangels, not even six!

In her workshop we used "angel cards", and I drew Gabriel with the aspect of "Ausdruck" which I translate to mean expression, or in my case self-expression, or creative expression such as through the writing of this book, or connected activities, and the colour of light blue, which for me means healing and inspiration. All summer I had found one reason after another for not writing any more of this book. I did not want to write it. Yet it is a form of self-expression, a book full of inspired "messages" from other realities and realms of consciousness, and Gabriel is the archangel who brought Mary the tidings of Jesus's coming birth, Gabriel the messenger of God.

We worked with "our" angels throughout the workshop, for each of us had picked one of these angel tarot cards. For those who have not done this, the cards are all laid face down on the floor, and in this case the question held in the mind while intuitively choosing a card was "Which one expresses what I most need to work on at the moment?" All of the cards had the name of an archangel, and which aspect of that angel was needed.

There was a little booklet to go with the cards which provided a few more details. I looked at the list of the names of the archangels, and saw with great interest that one of them was called ELOHIM. It did not take much for me to work out that the Elohim band of angels to whom I refer in the story, "Help from the

Elohim Angels" were obviously working under the leadership of the archangel Elohim, something that I did not know before.

When I arrived back in England, to my amazement I found that what I wanted to do most of all was to write more of this book. Gila with her 'energy work' and the angels together had helped me to move the blocks from my throat chakra, and had strengthened the connection between the throat chakra and my heart, the latter being a second place where my ability and desire for creative expression had been blocked. This was the seventh time that Michael and Gila had run this particular workshop.

I regard the archangels as facets of the God-energy. I see them as powerful thought forms of love who are capable of omnipresence, and therefore able to help all of us at once, and that none of us are too small or insignificant for them. Gabriel appeared to me as a being of great beauty and light wearing a many-pointed dazzling pale blue and white star on it's breast, and attired in long shining light creamy-gold coloured robes. I could not see boundaries to the aura of this archangel, as there seemed to be so much light everywhere. If Gabriel looked quite different when you saw it, I believe that that was Gabriel's choice, and that the experience was exactly right for you.

I call the angels 'its', because as far as I can tell they are neither male nor female. It is in no way intended to be disrespectful to them, and I am sure that they understand my difficulties in putting these stories into the best possible words. Even the colours round them often do not really fit any earthly description. I just do the best that I can.

7. Message From an Angel

This is my seventh angel story. It took place before any of the other six angel stories, but I choose to put it last in this chapter, because it touched me so deeply with its love, understanding, and simplicity. I would like it to touch the hearts of those who read it.

In 1988 I was participating in the "Light Workers Training" held in Hamburg, Germany, led by Rhea Powers and Gawain. It was the most beautiful May afternoon, and we were given some free time between sessions. I took myself into one of Hamburg's public Parks, and sat down on a bench to enjoy the sun and the scent of the flowers. As I closed my eyes, I saw an angel approaching. The part of me free of my body knelt down in front of the angel, who was showing me something in the palm of its hand. I looked. It was a replica of the legendary Lincoln Imp.

This little imp was reputed to have climbed up one of the stone columns in Lincoln's beautiful cathedral in an attempt to join the angels high up at the top of these in the place known as the 'Angel Choir'. As it reached the feet of the angels, it was turned into stone as a punishment for coming too close to them. Now both imp and angels are carved in the stone masonry for everyone to see. I was told about this legend as a small child when my mother took my sister and me to see the cathedral. Somewhere it had made a deep impression on my childlike mind, and I had treated angels with the greatest of respect ever since, even though I never really believed that they would turn me into stone if I misbehaved.

So there I was on my knees with my gaze fixed on this little stone imp in the hand of the angel. Then something wonderful happened. As I watched, I saw the imp transformed into a living and beautiful pale pink rose in full bloom. The flower, which looked so vulnerable, was a symbol of love. Then the angel took me gently by the hands and raised me to my feet. My fear was gone, and from that moment on I understood that the angels did not want me to be afraid of them, but to relate to them like friends. They had more love than I had ever dared to dream about.

Chapter 8

Hedgehogs

This communication came to me during one of my meditations at home with my friend Margot on 6th. August, 1994. I saw a hedgehog who apparently was stuck inside a glass bottle. It appeared to be trying to get out through the bottle neck, but of course its mature body was too big for more than the end of its nose to enter the bottle neck. I answered its unspoken question by saying, "Well, how did you get into the bottle?" The little fellow turned around, and walked out of the broken end of the bottle, which I had been unable to see before. I noticed how he scratched his little feet on the sharp edges, as I realised that some thoughtless human had thrown the broken bottle down on a rubbish heap without considering the nasty cuts that it might cause to any visiting wild life. With bleeding feet the hedgehog hurried away.

Now I was looking at Mrs. Hedgehog with a little family of four young following her one behind the other. I was shown fencing posts being driven into the ground, and strands of barbed wire being used. All sorts of man-made barriers were being erected over the land. Mrs. Hedgehog kept finding that her path was barred, and seemed to be making small circles in her endeavours to find a safe haven for her young. They looked such harmless little creatures, and the message I was receiving from them seemed to say that they wanted mankind to think of them more, to be considerate, and take the needs of the hedgehogs into account when throwing out their rubbish, and blocking hedgehog highways, for the hedgehogs have as much right to be here as we have.

Weeks later on 16th. September, I decided I must add something to this account. I had visited my mother the previous week-end, and spotted some information on wild life in her sitting room. It was just something that had been sent to her free through the post as part of an advertisement, but, there on top of a pile of papers, was a picture of a hedgehog . I picked it up, and on turning the page, I saw to my excitement a picture of mother hedgehog followed by a family of four young in single file behind her. This was really interesting for me, as before I had the vision, I had no idea if a hedgehog had ten babies or one, or whether or not they would follow her.

The next event of interest was when I picked up one of the free newspapers that comes through my door once a week, and just as I was about to put it unread on the pile for recycling, I saw a headline "Be kind to Pricklies." I wondered what on earth 'Pricklies' were, and peeped inside to read on. It turned out that they meant hedgehogs, and were warning people about the damage that carelessly thrown out broken glass, plastic bags, and especially the plastic rings that hold four cans together, as well as other rubbish can cause to them.

Chapter 9

Polar Bears

On 7th. January 1994 when meditating at home, I saw a polar bear, as white as they come on the snow-covered ice. He looked at me, and moved on. I had been expecting a message, as usually the animals come for a reason. Darkness fell on my inward eye, but just as I was thinking I had lost the link with the bears, I saw several of them on the ice. There was a big one with its nose pushed down inside an old discarded tin scrounging food. I saw the danger of the tin getting stuck on the end of its nose, as he had had to push so hard to reach the food scraps at the bottom. Also it was sharp, and could cut him. There were baby bears as well. One of the adults stood up on its hind legs, and looked round at me. I detected an uneasiness amongst the bears. I could see that they were close to a settlement of humans, and that destiny brought them ever closer together. This was a real cause for concern. The bears' natural curiosity was leading them into unnecessary danger. That alone would bring them too close to the men, even without the possibility of finding food there. This was shown to me not just by feelings, but also by a picture of a bear standing on the ice with a narrow strip of water between his ice and the ice where the humans were. The two ice masses drifted together to join up, and I saw horror and fear in the bear's expression as it shrank back from the closing gap. I felt that bears and humans are not very compatible, and that they were happiest when each species could keep to their own domain.

That was what I saw, and it felt like a cry for help from the bears. The wild-life documentaries that I have seen support the story of the bears, although one of the film crews had found a very successful solution. They encountered bears who had had no previous experience of mankind, and achieved a peaceful and happy co-existence by never going near the animals with any food, and also making sure that the bears never had access to their food supplies or left-over food, or rubbish. Therefore the bears could live close beside them without either species being a danger to the other. Those men understood what the bears wanted from them. I saw that film about a month after the vision.

Chapter 10

Ascended Masters, the Earth and the Sun

When I wrote about the archangels, I never listed their names, or discussed the possibility that there might be nine of them, not seven. I never went down the list describing the attributes of each one. There is already a wealth of other literature that deals with all this. I could have looked it up and copied it, but that would completely defeat the object of this book which is to pass on my personal experiences, be they accurate or inaccurate, complete or incomplete. To me the rest of it is still just theory. True or untrue? I will know when I know it!

This is why, when I write about the Ascended masters, I am only passing on what I have experienced personally. That is my truth at this moment.

My first conscious meeting with the Ascended Masters in this lifetime.

My introduction to the Ascended Masters in this life-time took place on 31st. July 1982. At that time I was still a member of a local 'Spiritualist Church', a useful steppingstone along my spiritual pathway. The church held a development circle once a week, and having moved into temporary lodgings close by 15 days previously, I sought to continue developing my psychic talents by joining their circle. The purpose of this circle was to enable people to develop the art of channelling information or messages from deceased friends and relatives to the living, and by these means give evidence of life after death. Sometimes that was exactly what I found myself doing, but on this particular night my spiritual guides chose to work differently with me. I was shown a series of pictures, and each time that they knew that I had seen one of them correctly, a visible sign was given to me so that I would know that I had it right.

Having passed these tests, my guides decided that I was ready to be shown something else.

I saw shadowy or translucent figures with their heads slightly bowed as though they were in prayer or a deep meditation. There were about twelve or thirteen of them standing in a circle facing outwards. I could not count them up accurately, as I was unable to see the whole of the circle at any one time. There was a blueish misty light all round them. When I looked at the hair of one of them, I recognised him as the old man who I had seen two weeks before when he was reading a very old and enormous book of knowledge and/or wisdom, which I have since felt must symbolise the akashic records. He seemed to be both very wise, and knowledgeable, but still researching. I felt that these spirits had existed there for thousands of years, and that they were members of a band. It was just as though they were keeping an eye on the whole of creation, and active in a very still way. I felt that they were holding various energy forces in balance. I saw them in full length light blue robes. A bright light was shining onto the one I had recognised.

About two months later, I met someone who told me about the existence of the Ascended Masters, something I had never heard of before, but I was quite certain that that was what I had seen. "... about twelve or thirteen of them," she said to me.

More of the Ascended Masters

I could start the next story with something like, "I saw the Ascended Masters standing there in a circle." I considered that, but then I knew that I wanted to share the cleansing process that took place first. Just as I described George Pratt's method of leading us up a stairway and letting us shed a garment on every step, so that we did not take any of the ego or personality or negativity that we might have been wearing with us, in George's absence it is often the angels who take it upon themselves to clean me up. It is not always the same way. In fact it is almost always slightly different each time, but serves the same purpose. I am not sure why in this story I am so unsteady on my feet at the beginning, unless it is to show how support is there when I need it. Another lesson in trust.

On 7th. January 1994, when meditating at home with Margot, I saw a large round light bulb with the light on, and I noticed that the base of it was purple. (Power colour). Immediately I found that I was lying on a bed snug under the covers with two angels, one on either side of the bed at my head, and they were starting to lift me out of the bed, before helping me onto my feet beside it. It was as though I was very weak and unsteady on my feet, for they escorted me away supporting my body, one from either side to keep me upright. We travelled a little way like this, until we reached a place where one of the angels seemed to be supporting me, and the other one picked up a cake of creamy-white soap and rubbed it all over my body. Next we moved forwards a few steps to a place where, as we arrived, silvery-golden water or light showered down upon me as the angels washed me clean. Thus prepared, and with my naked form having turned a cleaner paler shade of cream, we proceeded. I was shown myself being given a microphone. There are many ways I could interpret this, but obviously in some way it is intended that my voice will be heard. (I just hoped that it did not mean television interviews, as I would feel totally unprepared to cope with those.)

The next phase of this trip was the sensation that we were travelling upwards through mists of a pale blueish hue. I found it a very sensual experience. My body felt very light and pleasantly streamlined, and I felt filled with light, perhaps one of the benefits of the light-shower that I had just received. Mostly in out-of-the-body experiences like this I lose any awareness of having a body, and am just like a piece of consciousness in space. but this time I was very body conscious, and delighted in the sensation of the breeze that seemed to blow around and almost through my relaxed and supple body as we travelled. I felt the supporting hands of the angels on my naked form as they guided me through space, and I pondered about the sensual enjoyment I was having. (I noted that in spite of my lack of clothes, there was not even the slightest suggestion of anything sexual.) There was the firm hand in the middle of my back that powered me through space, and also other bodily contact as though my awareness was being heightened. This part of the journey was completed as we reached a place where I recognised the Ascended Masters standing in a circle looking outwards just as I had perceived them before. I was drawn to one in particular, having first with their permission allowed my being to drift around within their circle, as though I needed to absorb some of the energies up there, as though I needed to get in touch again with some ancient knowledge that I had previously been in contact with. By now I did not have a body, but was just consciousness.

As I linked up with this great being (Master), he pointed very powerfully to something in the Universe. I travelled downwards to get a closer look at what was being indicated. I saw a planet bathed in blue. As I came closer I saw that it had many colours, and by now I had decided that this was probably Planet Earth. Moving past it in space, but close to it, was something like a shallow light blue disc. I cannot say for certain what this was, but perhaps a space-ship from another planet. Its texture had an unearthly quality about it. Either it was not truly dense as Earth-ships would be, or else it gave off this blue semi-solid light concealing its form.

Although I travelled through space amongst the stars, I felt that I must be missing something that I was supposed to see. Surely this was not all. What were they trying to show or tell me? Look and ask as I might, I could not find anything more satisfactory than the thought that the Ascended Masters were keeping a very close watch on Planet Earth. I felt that they did not interfere in any way with the events taking place. What ever was happening had to be allowed to happen. Interference from high places did not seem to be in keeping with the laws of creation, and yet it was as though they were waiting for an opening, as though at the right time in the right conditions they might have a larger part to play. As I write this, it comes to me that in spite of this they are always there in their place to inspire and assist mortals who reach out to them. They seem to hold a balance point in the Universe. This phase of my meditation broke off here. I assume it was complete.

The above account is exactly how I wrote it a day or two after it happened. I had completely forgotten the bit about the angel handing me a microphone near the beginning of it, and have just re-read that part including how I reacted to it then. It is now over a year later, the end of January 1995, and I am preparing myself to travel to Germany at the beginning of March to help make a film for a television documentary. Instead of running away from it as I might have done a year ago, I have a strong feeling that this interview is something that is right for me to do. How everything changes!

Channelling in France

From 24th. to 27th. February, I was enjoying the Light Institute's four "Advanced Sessions" with the help of Susan Harris in France. The first two days we were concentrating on my kundalini energy, and the second two days, having 'opened me up' (my words), the theme was channelling. We were open to anything that my Higher Self in its wisdom wanted me to channel, and therefore I had no preconceived ideas about who or what I would be channelling. Susan helped to direct it, almost fulfilling the role that the angels normally play in my visions, meditations, or channelling. Starting with the first of the two channelling days under Susan's guidance, it happened like this.

I was looking onto the surface of a planet. It had holes in the surface, which numbered about six, were round, and quite symmetrically placed. The atmosphere was not unlike that of the Earth I observed, but only after I had been there a little longer did I decide that it was the Earth. It was almost as though something was stored in the holes. Sometimes they were closed with lids over them, and sometimes they were open. They were situated on high ground not far from mountains or hills, and I felt that at some point in my life I would go to this place. I was shown that a kind of living creature dwelt in them. I continued to channel what came to me.

"The creatures in there are semi-physical. They look more like animals than people. They are whitish-grey. (Could be a transparent white, which looks greyish with the dark background of the rocks behind them.) They belong inside the Earth, but there has been some kind of intervention from humans, which may have disturbed their living place. They were discovered by accident. The openings/holes (with lids which appear to be man-made) are a cause of distress to them. They are not adapted to the open air, so they feel insecure. They live in dark tunnels under (in) the Earth. I am sending them a message to use this as an opportunity to evolve further, and to advise them to adapt to the changing conditions."

After moving my consciousness into one of them, this is how I experienced their consciousness.

"They have a very still sort of energy. Although they are semi-physical, they have the same sort of stillness as the rocks." (I have never felt even slightly like this as a human. It is like a totally different concept of time, and as though I am in as much hurry as a stone which lies still on the earth, and I feel like a stone in spite of the lack of density in the creature's body.)" Moving out of their consciousness again;

"They can see me, and perceive me not as a human, but as a light messenger. They have contact with the angels from time to time. They do hear my message, and they are going to make some of their holes deeper in the Earth for security. All communication with them is telepathic. No words, just passing ideas. They have understanding between one another and the rocks, and they know what to do. I have never felt an energy like theirs before, not in this lifetime.

Their purpose is to provide consciousness with another way of growing, experiencing, and evolving. They connect very closely to the rocks. They are adapting by learning to retreat further from the surface. It is better for them when men do not know that they are there, and that when men gather round to look at the holes, they see nothing.

70

The creatures are much closer to the mineral kingdom than the animal kingdom. They don't need to move very fast, but they are experiencing the understanding with the rocks, and they feel the energies of the planet all around them. They are close to the crust of the planet."

I allowed my consciousness to merge with the consciousness of the creatures again, and continued.

"There is a lot of movement in the planet, the inside is not still. There is much more movement and change towards the centre than there is around its crust. The energies of the planet feel very very strong."

Without any prompting from Susan I found myself channelling the Planet Earth.

The Planet's Message

"I hurt. I am evolving, and although it is all very primitive, I provide a playground, a school for many forms of consciousness. For my consciousness to move closer to the light, it is necessary for the beings who inhabit the surface also to move towards the light. Otherwise, although space is an illusion, I feel partially separated from the light.

I participate, for I am not separate from the rest of consciousness. My actions mirror the actions of those around me. When there is anger, I show anger. When there is tranquillity and love, I show peace and harmony.

I hurt.

I am not to remain in my present form for ever. I too inhabit a temporary physical body, but my life-span is longer than that of men, much longer, and I am not yet old."

At this point Susan was starting to say something, but the Planet had not finished.

"I wish to speak.

I give a lot of support to many life forms. I ask for love in return, that I too may be nourished."

I sent a gift of light to the Planet, many times tinged with the soft pink of love. Then I saw the planet enclosed in clouds of soft pink light.

When I thought about the "creatures" channelled in this session, I remembered how once when I was abroad, I had had the vision of one of them rising up out of the rocks and showing itself to me. Then the vision faded leaving me wondering what on earth it was that I had seen. Another time I was looking at some postcards of paintings by a visionary artist, and saw a perfect portrait of one of these creatures, but I never managed to find out what it was. This was important evidence for me of the reality of their existence. He had painted it the same ghostly white with its long thin neck on a small four-legged body. I perceive these animals as being quite big.

Now I come to the second channelling day in France. Everything, every word, in all of these sessions was meticulously written down by Susan Harris to whom I am deeply grateful. That way, only things that I saw but forgot to mention at the time could possibly get missed out or wrongly remembered, but I tried very hard to say all of it. When putting these stories from sessions into a book, if the English is very bad, I edit it. For example "My head is square. Oh! Some kind of knob on the back of it. Next bit not clear. Oh yes! Think that eyes are kind of blue, has slit down centre, head that is. Is sort of, kind of, well yes squarish, but knob funny shape." etc. needs re-writing in my opinion! That was a made up example, and as far as I know it never happened! However, I would like the first paragraph of the next section to be written just as I said it, (there might be a very little editing done when I copied Susan's notes, but very little) so that you can share the experience with me more deeply just as it took place.

After some preparation, Susan asked me which part of my body my attention was drawn to.

"Attention drawn to "dwelling place of God" (just below throat on either side) and the neck. It looks like an open channel of light. I am looking at my throat chakra, like a flower with many petals. I see white, and a rich violet colour around the edge. The energy is moving outwards. It goes through sky-blue into my head. I feel heat around my ears, especially on the right side. Looking in my head, I see red and blue, quite active in there. I see red and blue and white. They are vibrating, moving into crown chakra. Everything seems to be going upwards. There is a shaft of light going out of the top of my head. It stretches up. It reaches a long way up to a place of a beautiful shade of blue. There is also a lot of white and golden light. A lot of angels flying around.

I am looking at this shaft of white light. It is reaching up through this realm, the light gets brighter and brighter. There are other beings up there. They look like masters. They are reminding me that I have seen them before. (This was the first time that I had seen them together since 31/7/'82.) There are about 12 of them in a circle.

I see them as having eyes with great depths. I see one of them like a mother figure, female. Very deep blue (robes), and very kind eyes. Light shines out of them.

I feel that the consciousness of these beings has always been. It is ageless. I feel that they are actually much bigger than the forms that I see. They are looking out like guardians of the Universe. I feel that they are able to see, to penetrate with their consciousness the most distant places without moving. They understand the illusion of space. They can see all of time."

When Susan asked me to enter the consciousness of one of them, I hesitated, but when one of them beckoned to me, I knew that I was to share consciousness with him. He told me not to be afraid. The first thing that struck me was his vision. When I was looking out through his eyes, it was with very strong penetrating shafts of golden light that could pierce infinity. With these eyes he could look at any point in time that he wished. He was almost like a time machine.

He showed me a place on Earth where there was a gathering of people. They looked like the Romans of ancient times. They were wearing long whitish robes, and some kind of head-dress which only partially covered their heads. All men, they stood outside a temple which had columns of a light cream colour along the front of it. The sun was very strong. They were sun-worshippers connecting with the sun. The consciousness of the sun is very powerful, and it spoke to them.

The Ascended Master asked me to listen to what the sun had to say to us now.

THE SUN: It feels that many of us have forgotten that the sun too has a consciousness. It has wisdom and power, and it used to be of service to mankind through the connecting of its consciousness with that of mankind. But now we don't hear it any more, because most of us could not believe that the sun could speak intelligently to us. We are closed. The sun calls us to open our hearts.

The Sun says, "The Earth is not a planet on its own. It is connected in so many ways to so many other planets and lifeforms in the Universe. Those living on the Earth are as part of the Earth. It is not beneficial either to planet Earth, or to the rest of the Universe for this planet to be in any way closed off from the rest of creation. The Earth does not even provide its own light, so how can it see itself as a separate entity. We are all part of one whole. The smallest little insect is part of that whole. Nothing is self-sufficient. The Earth-people forget this."

The following morning at breakfast, another person there (in France) for sessions told me that she remembered reading about a 'sun-cult' in Egypt for whom peace had reigned for one thousand years. I cannot rule out the possibility that the men I saw might have been in Egypt, and not Italy, but I do not know.

The Energy Net

Since doing these sessions, I have heard someone else talk of an energy net around the earth, so as this 'other life' that I spontaneously drifted into speaks of something like this, and also I rather enjoyed the life, I am including it here.

Other Life

I remember long ago, when Planet Earth was still young, I and my kind were like free roaming specks of consciousness that travelled the galaxy. We were little creatures whose job it was to help with the connections. I saw myself playing with strands of energy connecting them up from one place to another place, until the whole Universe looked like a giant spider's web. We were small and green, but the Earth men (if they were there then, for they may have just arrived) would not have been able to see us with their physical eyes, for we were of a different vibration. I enjoyed my work. We were green round the outside, and white in the middle, and pulsated with life. I was an expert traveller. I moved at the speed of my thoughts, so any distance could be covered in an instant. I was permanently tuned in to a consciousness that was above all consciousness. By this means I always knew where I was most needed.

In my head, I reached out with my energy-like antennae to connect, and feel where I was drawn. I remember how I enjoyed sliding down a ray of sunshine. It was like a game.

The Council of Animals

Shortly after reliving the life as a little green thing, I found that I was observing various changes and developments in my own energy field which had been brought about by the work in the sessions. While looking at it, I noticed that I was not the only observer. Higher above my head I saw The Council of Animals all looking down a funnel-shaped shaft of light that was coming from the top of my head, opening out as it went upwards. They had formed a circle round what appears to be the top of it, and were looking with great interest to see how much it had opened up. The giraffe stretched his long neck down inside it to get a better closer view. When they had all had a look, and made a note of what was going on, they wandered slowly away.

I thought they had all gone until I spotted a little bluebird sitting on top of my head pecking at it wanting to open up my channelling centres still further. A mermaid was also taking an interest in the proceedings, but saying that the light up above my head was too hot for her, she dived into some water to cool off. Next I realised that I could still see the elephant looking at the expansion above my head. He could hardly believe his eyes! They grew bigger and bigger. He touched me affectionately with his trunk. Susan had worked very well with me!

If I am to believe what the Animal Council has many times told me, which is that part of my role on the Earth during this lifetime is to speak for them, then it is very natural that they should be present like this, and taking a keen interest in my development as a channel. If I am to be one of those serving them this way, then they clearly want me to become as good a channel as it is possible for me to be. My progress is being closely watched!

At the end, while Susan was busy doing something with my aura, I saw other animals walking around the table on which I was lying, including a beautiful long-haired snow white cat. I am interested that such a cat should have come, because since then I have had a vision of a possible future for me in which a long-haired and very special white cat might be sharing the house with me. I am always suspicious of long-haired cats or dogs on the grounds that such a long coat must make excellent housing for a very large number of fleas, but perhaps I will get over that eventually.

What About Planet Earth?

In the fourth angel story of chapter seven, I only told part of the first meditation, as I wanted to include the rest later. 'Home', the place I was to travel to, definitely was not Planet Earth on this occasion. It was a beautiful state of being in the centre of a gently pulsating spherical light energy mass. The centre of it was perfect peace and stillness, and I took what seemed the natural course of gliding smoothly through its outer layers to rest in the still centre for a while. Even when it pulsated like a heart beat, the centre remained unmoved. A little of the outer layers seemed to be shed and released into space with every pulsation. The result of this was allowing little by little some of its own expanding consciousness to travel into the empty darkness and fulfil some purpose far away.

As I moved outwards towards its outer edges, I reached a place with enough activity to find out what I first heard about the Earth before I ever went there. Part of my consciousness travelled out through time and space on a research trip to have a look at it. "It's very slow" was my immediate reaction. Next I perceived myself holding the Earth in my hands, and then at the same time as pushing a key down into it from the north pole saying "It needs winding up. It needs loving. It needs music." I could see that it needed many of us to go and gather round it to love it and quicken its vibrations. I was asked to go and help. (I do not know by whom. Maybe it was a spiritual guide, or even my own higher self.)

(After note, January 1995. This would hardly be an unselfish mission, as it would greatly benefit my own evolution, and as I would need many lives on Earth in order to learn enough about it, I would experience darkness, and not only the light, and my soul would grow wiser.)

The men who I saw on Earth had forgotten that they were a part of God. They were lost. They were searching for God in their religions and their churches, but they never looked where God resided, within, in their own hearts. They were ignorant of many things, and because of this and increasing technological advancement, they were destroying themselves and the planet. Their values were out of line with the divine consciousness. They were sleeping. That is to say that the God in them was sleeping, and was not expressed, for they were no longer aware of it. They needed to wake up, and remember again. That the planet needs music was repeated several times.

I was shown a picture of a group of men clustered together in the desert looking lost. I agreed to help, and remain until the problem had been resolved.

Regarding the last sentence of that account, I have heard from other teachers that none of us can go 'home' alone, but only when the very last of us is ready to come as well. Seen in that light, it makes helping other people or animals for example, (and they are definitely people) with their spiritual evolvement a very selfish task indeed. I must add that it is my belief that 'selfish' is not wrong in this context, so I do not mean that I think it is wrong to help others, but the opposite! One of the hardest things for me is not finding out what my truth is, but living it. Therefore I try to stop myself from preaching to others, with mixed success, as often as possible.

Chapter 11
Findhorn and the Fairies

On October 24th. of 1992 I went to Findhorn to spend a week learning T'ai Chi. Being an outdoor person, I made a point of finding time to go for walks in the woods and surrounding countryside every day, as well as attending the T'ai Chi classes.

One morning towards the end of the week, my walk brought me back to Cluny Hill College (where the Foundation was running its T'ai Chi course) by the gate at the bottom of the garden near the compost heap and the vegetable patch. I looked with interest to see what the gardeners were growing there, and noticed two orange things which looked like half oranges sitting on the earth. I remembered how my mother had taught me years before to leave the peel of half an orange like a little dome on top of the soil, so that slugs would collect underneath it, and could then be removed from the garden, and effectively prevented from eating bulbs and flowers that I was trying to grow. I knew that the Findhorn gardeners did not poison the earth with chemicals, and was filled with an overwhelming curiosity to find out how many slugs were gathering under the orange peel. I decided to move from my position on the garden path, and take a closer look.

Immediately I made this decision, I became aware of an energy force-field just in front of me which was desperately trying to block my way. My intuition told me that this was being put there by the garden fairies/nature spirits. (Pick which ever word fits in best with your personal belief system.) I felt a certain hostility towards my presence coming from these little beings on the other side of the forcefield. I had never been aware of nature spirits trying to hold me at bay before, even though I am a person who has wandered freely through many wild and beautiful places where one might expect to find them, and full of surprise, I wondered what on earth had happened to my energy field that they found me so undesirable. I stopped dead in my tracks, and respectful of their wishes, but undaunted, I put out the request telepathically, "Permission to enter for learning please." The reply "Permission granted." came quickly, and I felt the forcefield being removed, so I stepped forward to examine the orange-peel slug traps. As I came closer, I could see that it was not orange peel, but some kind of bright orange vegetable growing on the ground. I lifted one of them very carefully for closer inspection, and wondered if it could be a pumpkin. I had never seen them growing before, but when I asked someone the following day, it turned out that that is what they were. My mission accomplished, I departed from the vegetable garden, having first thanked the fairies for being agreeable to my visit.

At lunch-time I saw Sue, one of the gardeners, and wanted to share my experiences with her, but she was so deeply engrossed in conversation, first with one friend and then with another, that I did not like to interrupt them. So later in the day, when I found myself sitting next to Patricia, one of the facilitators for the T'ai Chi workshop, as I was still bursting with the desire to tell someone what had happened, I related my experiences in the garden to her. At the end of it she said, "You should tell the gardeners this. It would be helpful to them to know."

Late afternoon our little T'ai Chi group assembled as usual for thirty minutes of silent meditation in Cluny's Sanctuary. Something prompted me to tune in to the vegetable patch, even though I was not physically present there. Quite close to the compost heap end of it I saw an energy vortex. It looked like earth energies to me, and I remembered how I had learnt in Arizona that such places sometimes act as gateways for the coming and going of unseen beings of many kinds. I felt that from this one, things came from the depth of the earth that would normally not be nearly so accessible to the garden. They seemed to me to be earth energies with their own consciousness which could come and go there. The colour of this vortex was a brownish orange.

The evening came, and I made myself comfortable in the sauna, one of the luxuries of Findhorn. We had spent more of the day outside than usual, and after the cold late October wind blowing through me, the heat of the sauna was most welcome. There were about three of us enjoying it, but we were silent, which allowed me to stay with my own thoughts. It felt right to follow Patricia's advice, so I decided to get to work on manifesting a few moments alone with Sue, so that I could talk to her without any distractions. Shortly after that the other people in the sauna left. I was only alone in there for one or two minutes at the most. The door opened, and through it came Sue on her own. "Perfect," I thought to myself. "This is my golden opportunity."

"Sue! You are the very person whom I most wanted to see." I began, and followed this with the afore given account of the day's events. When I reached the bit about manifesting some time alone with her, she exclaimed, "But I hardly ever come into the sauna!" It turned out that her friend Lorraine had just talked her into it, so Lorraine had picked up the vibes as well.

Now it was Sue's turn to talk. She told me how about a year ago an Irish psychic had visited the garden, and told the fairies to go away. They obediently left, and Sue said that after this they (Sue and the other gardeners) had had a difficult time persuading the fairies to return. After they finally did get them back, they briefed them not to listen to anyone else's instructions but theirs, and it seems to me that they then understood that not everyone was to be welcomed, as some came with unconstructive ideas like "Let's get rid of the nature spirits." My communication that I had only wanted to learn must have reassured them that I was not a threat to be feared or avoided, so that they had dropped their defences, and watched to see what I would do. I had kept my side of the agreement which is probably why I had experienced them as playful and friendly before I left. Even if some of them were still keeping a respectful distance from me, the bolder ones had come quite close. So there was not, as I had feared, anything very wrong with my energy field.

Sue also told me that they knew about the energy vortex that I had perceived when meditating in the Sanctuary, which was useful confirmation for me that I had not accidently imagined it all.

The following day I told Patricia about my meeting with Sue, and she said, "But I've never seen her in the sauna!" which made that part of it all the more remarkable. I also noted that my conversation with Sue had reached its natural completion at exactly the right moment to allow me just the precise amount of time necessary to leave the sauna, have a shower, and get myself ready for the meeting of the T'ai Chi group at 8.00 p.m.. As I left the sauna, others arrived to go in, so the space in which to talk to Sue without interruption had been the exact length required, no more and no less. It is true Lorraine had been in there for the last couple of minutes, but then she had been the one to guide Sue in the required direction, and as I understood things, she was also connected to the garden.

On Friday morning I felt moved to visit the garden again. I approached the vegetable garden from the opposite direction this time. It is laid out like two small rectangles with high hedges around them, and a small gap in the hedge to allow movement from one to the other. As I arrived at the corner of the first one, not being sure if I had previously been granted a 'day-pass' or one that would last me for the whole week, I hesitated to try and feel whether or not there would be a force field there to discourage entry. I was just thinking, "Well I can't feel anything," when I clearly heard "Enter!" coming from the fairies/nature spirits. This time I had no sense of hostility, and I knew that they had remembered me from the previous day. I reverently walked through the first of the rectangular plots, looking at the vegetables as I went.

On reaching the gap in the hedge leading to the second plot, I paused, wondering if this would count as separate territory, or part of the same area. I heard "Please enter. Be at peace with us." Now I felt welcomed rather than just tolerated. I looked around at the healthy vegetables, and then standing close to the energy vortex, I decided to take my leave of the garden and its fairies. I acknowledged them with a small gesture of my hands, thanking them for the blessing of the harmony and understanding that now reigned between us. Their reaction really touched me. "No one has done that to us for ages!" they cried out joyfully, as though their worth was rarely recognised. I suspected that they had forgotten to include Sue and her friends, or that they meant "No one who is not directly involved in working with us has done that for ages!" Whether "ages" means half an hour, or several weeks, or ten or more years is another debatable point, but the wish and longing of these little people to be taken into account during our interactions with Mother Nature was crystal clear to me.

Chapter 12

Prehistoric Animals, and Visitors to the Young Planet

In May of 1993 I went to Mexico to join Chris Griscom's workshop on the theme of "Dolphins and Extraterrestriality."

On the first day we worked through various issues with the help of our inner-child. My inner-child was having one of her more active days, and chose to show me many things. It is possible that she was led by the angels, for she found much to reveal and share with me outside our immediate relationship with each other. This chapter is to contain the parts of this sharing that I consider to be of interest to others.

After being led through pathways of light which had little bubbles of light around them, the bubbles being a type of energy that contributed to making up this particular dimension that we were visiting, and on the way connecting with a lion (that is the energy of the lion in a place of light with a little red and orange around it), we reached a place where my attention was drawn to an area on my right. At first I just perceived that the area was very green, then that it had something to do with some type of animal consciousness, and then as things came into a clearer focus I could see that they bore little resemblance to the animals we know on Earth today, for they were prehistoric animals. This was/is a timeless place where they always exist. I saw trees as well as many other life-forms there.

The message from the animals was that in this timeless place they have always been. First they were here/there, then they evolved on Planet Earth, and now they are still there/here. The place exists outside time and space as we know them, and therefore it is very difficult to find the right words and tenses in which to talk about it, especially as during my session I came from a moment in 1993. I apparently went somewhere else to visit them, and arrived in a dimension that seemed to be both here and somewhere else, and still only in one place, outside time, and yet with its own time that is different to ours and timeless. The animals explained that their destiny and evolution on the Earth was all planned beforehand, as was their departure when the right time for that arrived. Their consciousness, the God within, was finding ways of experiencing itself in matter.

My inner child took me down a tunnel-like path. It must have been a passageway through time. At the other end I saw no animals, just a barren Earth. I looked further, and saw the young Earth with life-forms arriving in the form of vegetation. The angels were looking at the planet. She was beautiful, new, young, and a virgin planet. I could see all around her, and how in the astral many beings or potential life-forms were admiring her, and lining themselves up for the possibility to incarnate here and colonise the planet. The planet herself was conscious, and already housing many forms of consciousness in the rocks. I felt that she was feminine, because she seemed to be giving birth to so many life-forms. Some of them were a selection of extraterrestrial beings who just wanted to merge their consciousness with that of the rocks, others with that of the water. They wanted to merge with and experience the energies here.

The first trees were coming. Many of the E.Ts. were regarding them in wide-eyed wonder. Many different forms of life were arriving to colonise land, air, and water; but not all of them were totally physical. Many of the E.T. visitors were experiencing the Earth in semi-physical forms or bodies. Some of them dwelt in caves amongst the rocks. With so many galactic entities arriving at the same time, there was already competition amongst them regarding who should colonise the Earth. I saw that the seeds of disharmony were already being sown.

They came from many different parts of the galaxy, and some from even further away. Some just stayed for a short while to experience this planet, and then returned from whence they came, whereas others came to stay more permanently.

At this point I became in touch with a past life at that time. It is likely that we had not really achieved living as individuals in the way that people do now, but were more of a group spirit, for I recalled things almost as though I were the group, or the higher consciousness/soul of the people.

My inner-child showed me how I was one of these early settlers, and how having come from a non-physical planet, we had difficulty trying to penetrate this dimension, and trying to materialise ourselves in a physical way on this physical planet. Not all of our attempts were successful.

In this way, however, it was possible to colonise Planet Earth without first evolving through other life-forms here. We were not descended from apes or monkeys. Sometimes it was very hard for us to be here, as it was like a culture shock. It took us a long time to slow the energy down enough for it to form matter. Some of our unsuccessful attempts resulted in bodies with some less dense areas, and patches that were over dense like hard little lumps. We spent many hundreds of years on Earth perfecting this art, until with our thoughts we could control it quite well.

Some of us became lost in physicality, forgetting who we were; while others retained the connection and knowledge of where we came from, and they learned to materialise and dematerialise, and even to bi-locate.

When the physical dimension was established, I and others like me left the planet. Those who were left behind were the ones who chose to continue the early colonisation of Planet Earth. We returned to the planet that we had come from. It was a beautiful blue colour, and there we re-established ourselves for a while before we felt ready to visit other dimensions again.

Chapter 13
Dolphins In Mexico

During the "Dolphins and Extraterrestriallity" workshop that I referred to in chapter twelve, we not only tuned into the dolphin energy during each of our four Light Institute sessions, but we also went swimming with dolphins in the ocean a short drive away from where we were staying twice during the week. This chapter is about the information gleaned from my four sessions, the experiences that I had in the water with dolphins during the two swims, the information that Chris contributed through her personal observations which she passed on to us, and a brief account of a personal experience that took place on the beach afterwards.

In my first session in the morning of the first day, I felt quite apprehensive about channelling dolphin information as I knew very little about them, and was concerned that I might channel at least some of it wrong. So in the evening I studied the morning's notes to try and see which points that had come up had any relevance to the 'Dolphin Swim' in the afternoon.

In my session I had experienced myself beneath the surface of the water watching and feeling the white under-side of a dolphin as it slid smoothly up the whole length of my trunk, giving me the sensation of being stroked. This was very sensual, and drew up my kundalini energy. I saw the dolphin swimming around me saying, "You should enjoy that!" I did. My body felt very receptive to it, and it gave me the most amazing feeling of well-being, as though I were half way to a more ecstatic state. My cells were being fed with vital energy, and it helped to connect my awareness with the whole of my body. I was very conscious of the effect of being in water. The dolphins knowing this added, "Part of our state of consciousness is brought about by the water around us. It is lovely, because one is a little free from gravity." They continued, "When you swim with us later today, we would like you to put your heart and soul into enjoying us. We are there for you."

In the afternoon swim following this session, I was very relieved to see that the bottle-nosed dolphins did have very light coloured under-sides, almost white. This point alone helped me to accept the rest of the information as real, although, of course, I could prove nothing.

Next there was the instruction that the dolphins had given me about putting my heart and soul into enjoying them when I swam with them. I certainly did my best, and the highlight was when we came to the point in our swim when one at a time we were to be pushed through the water by two dolphins, each with its nose (I think that the noses are called beaks) pressed against the sole of one of our feet for one length of their lagoon. I went first. I had no idea what to expect, as I had not seen anyone do it before me. At first I was not clear which way up I should be, but I finally got into position on my tummy, so the signal was given for the dolphins to go to me. I am not sure if I had the full quota of two dolphins, or if one of them was not really pushing, but with my feet much too close together, I was pushed slowly in a very small half circle.

The girl organising the swim called out, "No, no! You are supposed to be facing the other way. I explained rather weakly that the dolphins had turned me round. I lined myself up for a second attempt, and without realising it, I corrected the positioning of my feet by putting them wider apart, which made it much easier for the dolphins to take me in a straight line. This time I felt a good even pressure on both feet, and the three of us set off at the most amazing pace in a straight line through the water. I had been having some difficulty holding my head end above the water while waiting for them, but just like a speed boat, I found that the whole of my front end began to rise up out of the water as we gathered speed. I did not know that my arms were supposed to be behind me to comply with the accepted method of doing this, so they were up in the air stuck out in front of me, which did not seem to matter as far as the dolphins were concerned. The sensation reminded me of waterskiing, only it was not the judgement and skill of the speed boat driver that I had to trust, but that of two dolphins in the water behind me. I was very aware of the three of us doing something together.

Although I had been in the water with the dolphins for some time now, this was the first moment where I really felt connected to their consciousness. I felt so strongly the presence of two "beings" behind me, and it felt like a close and trusting connection to two people, but they were in charge, thus the need to trust them. My trust was further tested as we approached the end of their enclosure with absolutely no sign of any reduction in speed, and I began to ask myself if they had realised that something was in the way, and how hard would I hit it. Then the whistle was blown for them, and they dropped me so suddenly that I met the end of the pool perfectly. I began to realise that I could really trust the situation. I turned myself round expecting that I was about to make a return trip. I lay ready in the water, but nothing was happening. "Aren't they going to take me back again?" I shouted out with tones of imminent disappointment.

Before the girl could explain to me that it was supposed to be a one way trip, I felt the two dolphin noses connect with my feet, and we were racing through the water again. As we neared the other end, the dolphin on my left foot started to push a little harder, so that they turned me quite beautifully in the direction of the steps where I could climb out of the water, and they would each receive a fish for their work. However, when we stopped, they stayed beside me just long enough for me to be able to turn round and stroke each of them once as a thank you before they left. "You are only supposed to go one way!" called the girl from across the water. "I am very sorry, I did not know," I replied, as I inwardly registered that I had just had double my money's worth, and no one had been able to prevent it! I was truly thankful that I had not known "the rules".

I knew that the dolphins had perfectly understood what I wanted from them, as they broke their usual routine, by failing to go and collect their fish after my first length! At least I don't think they had.

Meanwhile my whole relationship to them had altered to one of greater trust. When I climbed into the water with them at the beginning, they looked so unlike the horses that I was accustomed to dealing with, that I felt unsure how best to relate to them, or how to interpret their behaviour. In spite of this, when I stroked them, (as we had been advised to because they like it,) I was instantly in raptures over the wonderful texture of their silky soft skin, and fascinated to see how four large powerful dolphins managed to swim through the narrow gaps between the maze of swimming legs of the six humans without hurting any of us. My uncertainty concerning how to relate to them was particularly apparent when two of them came over to me and both of them nudged me on the chest quite firmly. I did not know if this was friendship or aggression, and had no idea how to deal with it. However, the dolphins had their own solution for that, and moved away.

Afterwards, in question and answer time with Chris, we asked her what she had experienced with their behaviour. She had noticed that the dolphins had sonared each one of us when we got into the water, and then saw that they were going round giving healing. They had assessed each person with their sonar, so they knew exactly what each one of us needed. Some of their little pushes with their noses were very precisely positioned to stimulate what ever part of our bodies they considered needed it. Therefore I determined that the next time I would take very careful note of where exactly they touched me. One of the men had had a bad back, and Chris saw a dolphin swim round behind him and prod him in the back exactly where the trouble spot was. When a disabled child (a very small boy) was held by his father and mother in the water, the dolphins were fascinated, and spent much time there, and showed great gentleness with him.

Chris Griscom said that these dolphins were there 'on call' for us by their own choice, a view with which I agree. It reminded me of the statement I had received from them in my morning session, "We are there for you!" The last part of the dolphin swim act consisted of the six of us forming a human chain treading water and holding hands while the dolphins approached from in front of us, swam under us, jumped out of the water just behind us, flew through the air above us, dived back into the water just in front of us, and were under us and jumping up behind us again to land in front of us a second time before swimming away. With both jumps, they passed so close behind us that they almost touched us as they left the water, but the second jump comes so much sooner than I expected it to due to their amazing speed through the water, that I was left in a very elated and excited state. I noticed that after the dolphin swims, everyone seemed to be on a real high, with shining eyes and happiness radiating out of them. Putting my heart and soul into enjoying them had not been very difficult.

The night following this first session and first dolphin swim, I awoke while it was still very dark, and as I lay there in the darkness, I became aware of a dolphin swimming past me, and at the same time I felt this pulsating in my head that seemed to come from the contact with the dolphins. I saw it as a piece of pale blueish pulsating light stretching through my head just above the level of my eyes. It felt like some kind of expanded consciousness, or as though I were developing some new type of awareness, or sensory ability. This occurred again in my third session.

The Second Dolphin Swim went as follows.

By this time, I had had my second, third, and fourth sessions, with a little part of each spent tuning into the dolphin energy. In the water I felt much bolder, and far more at home with them. I was determined to notice where exactly they touched me this time. The first contact was half way down my rib-cage on the left side. Chris said afterwards that there is an acupressure point there which helps the immune system. It was a very deliberate thrust with the end of its nose. Maybe this was to help my immune system, but I cannot rule out the possibility that the dolphin thought I should be stroking its tummy instead of lying there in the water pretending that I was a dolphin, or more accurately, trying to mimic their rolling action in the water to see if they were interested. I wanted to play!

The next point to be touched was under the left armpit. This was done so purposefully and accurately, that I felt sure the dolphin knew exactly where it wanted to touch me. Chris said that this point would affect the lymphatic system, and also help to keep me healthy. That was all that that particular dolphin wanted to do just then, because instead of rolling over to have its tummy stroked afterwards, mission accomplished, it swam away.

The third point was my throat, just where that little indentation is at the bottom of the neck at the front. This was the moment where I really benefited from what Chris had told us about the healing she had seem them giving out. I had at least three times the amount of trust this time. So I kept very still, stroked the dolphin gently, and waited a while, as it continued to hold its nose very gently just in contact with my throat. The dolphin and I both had to move a tiny bit in order to stay afloat, but we maintained this delicate contact in spite of that. This was quite unlike the other "prods" I had received, which were more momentary. Also it was one of the places where a dolphin had touched me in my second session. Afterwards Chris suggested that stimulating me here (throat) was very significant in view of my first book coming out, as I would need to increase my powers of communication.

During this second swim, I found that trying to be aware of where the dolphins were in the water without sonar was quite difficult. Even though they had auras and were bigger than us, I still found that they could arrive un-noticed behind me until they made one of their calls, or surfaced to take another breath of air sounding so like a human gasping for breath after diving, that I always had to turn round and look to see which of the two it was. I was keen to know where they were so as not to be taken by surprise, which I often was, and also to make it easier not to accidently kick them. In spite of what seemed a low level of awareness to me when I was in the water, I noticed on a number of occasions afterwards that I was more successful in crowds at moving around the other people, and anticipating their moves.

In my third session, I had tuned in to the experience of three dolphins moving in perfect unison with each other. I had particularly wanted to experience something like that. My chance came when we got to the 'push' part of the swim. Instead of the dolphins taking equal contact with my feet, the one on the right only touched me enough to let me know that it was there, but then seemed to deliberately miss my foot. So, as I could not see it, I found myself trying to feel its presence, and intuitively move my foot around in the water until I made contact with its nose. Meanwhile, the left hand dolphin only pushed very very gently, so that it effectively waited until I had established my rapport with the other one before getting up speed. One of my wishes had been to turn a corner while travelling this way. I noticed that we were making a smooth curve to the left. Then the direction changed, and we curved back to the right, thus finishing at the 'proper' place at the far end. Also we travelled at a slower pace, which had two advantages. Firstly, it was much more comfortable for the soles of my feet, and secondly, it gave me time to balance myself in the water, and adjust to the changes of direction as we made them. As usual, the dolphins were in charge. Again we were working together.

Finally one of my greatest wishes was granted. The swim was officially over, and I was just swimming towards the steps to get out for the last time when I met a dolphin. As it passed I reached out to give it a loving, but non-holding embrace, and as it slipped gently through my arms the whole length of its beautiful sensual body swept lightly against mine. It felt like the most loving and beautiful moment of the whole swim, seconded only by the sustained contact with my throat. Chris said that the dolphins knew exactly what we all needed, and this showed me that they certainly knew what I wanted. This was the same wonderful body to body contact which I have already described that I had experienced in another dimension during my first session, which is how I knew that I wanted to feel it with my physical body as well.

Going back to my sessions, it is only now in December of 1995 that I am beginning to realise how accurate and valid the dolphin information in them is. What brought me to these realisations I will explain in a later chapter.

In my second session I saw a dolphin straight in front of me with rainbow colours all around it. It began to spin anticlockwise around my body, flapping its tail about near my feet and ankles, thus stimulating my energy field with its energy field, so that my energy was rising upwards again. I felt its fins flapping around my face, around my nose, and received the message that I was to wake up. I felt its body against mine, again very sensual. It continued moving and spinning around me, and indicated an energy point on the lower right side of my belly, where I sensed something (energy) being put in there to make it spin faster, and then the same experience on the other side. The dolphin was now behind me, stimulating my body with physical contact. I was touched all over. Then it swam around my waist, through my legs from behind, and then up in front of me tapping me on the throat, the chin, and the third eye with its beak.

I saw a white energy that is flowing in and out of the cosmos, and I heard the dolphins saying that the humans have been sleeping, and that it is time for them to wake up. Meanwhile the white energy was starting to flow down my energy meridians. It was like water flowing down a new river-bed, as though my body had not had this type of energy before. The dolphins told me that it would heighten my sensitivity, that my physical senses would be sharpened, including the ones that I did not know I had. One of these would be my ability to tap into the feelings of the creatures around me, whether animal or human etc..

Next I saw a dolphin swimming along the surface of the water with a white patch of light at a particular point on its head. I followed the light from the dolphin's head to see where it was coming from, and found that it was linking it up with other realities including the sun. It seems that the connection with the sun gives them a sense of time, for I was shown a clock face with a whole series of numbers which did not have a clear meaning for me, as they came in a random order, or so it seemed.

The dolphins told me that they were very much affected by planetary movements, the activities of sun, moon, and stars. They are very sensitive to the different energies that these movements bring about. This affects the timing of daily actions like mating, etc.. They say that I will always be affected by the sun, the moon and the stars. (Obviously that goes for all life on Earth. I did not take it to mean that I was the only one!)

The dolphin showed me what it was doing with me in visual terms that I could understand. That is, it arrived with something like a straight stick in its teeth, which was then dropped down through my crown chakra, as though to clear out the energy pathways making more room for the energy to flow. I felt as though I was being flushed out with white light, which not only cleansed me, but made me feel more connected to other energies and this planet. I was learning from the dolphin consciousness how different the energies of the sun and the moon feel. They learn to recognise the different energies that the planets give off. Each has its own code, its own vibration, quite different from each other. At that point in my session, I felt I too could sense the different energies, even though I had not learned which was coming from where. They felt that I could learn which energies could be used for what, and told me how it was with exactly the same sensory equipment that I could sense the different energy fields of people, animals, trees, plants, places, and rocks. This sensory equipment senses vibration, which made it feel quite easy. (At least that it how it was in the session!)

In the third session (already referred to) it went like this. I saw two dolphins in the water in front of me facing me with their heads up. I watched them catching fish, one of which was passed to a younger dolphin. There was a male and a female. The male brushed his body lightly against the under-side of the female, and seemed to be trying to excite her a little. She returned his touch, obviously enjoying it. This was sensual.

Then there were three dolphins swimming parallel to one another, and it struck me that their consciousness was so connected that they swam as though they were one being. It was impossible when they changed direction to see any one of them turn before the others. My consciousness was drawn into theirs so that I could experience this. It felt like being in a current of water, and allowing the current to carry one. It felt like surrender. It was something very close to telepathy.

In the fourth and last session, I tuned into the dolphin energy again. A large dolphin appeared face to face with me, first touching me on the nose with his beak, and then giving me a powerful thrust in the solar plexus. Then some information about dolphins was imparted to me. I saw a lot of pulsating light in the dolphins' heads. Light of too high a frequency for the human eye to perceive radiated out from them. They can see auras, their own as well as ours. They are emotional with heart energy, and have good communication with each other. The third eye is well developed, and the openness of the crown chakra enables them to slip in and out of their bodies very easily. They have a chakra system extending well above their heads consisting of at least fifteen major ones. There are seven or eight of these closely aligned with the body, and the rest of them further away extending upwards beyond their heads. The lower chakras are rather like ours, and the ones above the head are more for things like long range perception, telepathy, reaching out through the rest of the galaxy to other dimensions like antennae, which includes another place where dolphins exist like a parallel reality to the Earth, and also to a place like a memory storehouse for dolphin genetics where they can be referred to in the event of dolphins having left this planet. For this reason the continued existence of dolphins is not in the hands of mankind.

To complete this session, there was an exchange of light and colours between the dolphins and me, which I experienced as a useful and loving inter-species communication.

I have not attempted to analyse or further interpret the meanings of these interesting events referred to in this chapter from my dolphin sessions, and the truth in them cannot be proven, only felt, so I have left it to each reader to accept what feels right to him or her, and to leave the rest or just enjoy it.

The other dolphin experience that I had came quite unexpectedly. I had been having a mildly frustrating time, because as it was known that I had written a book about what the animals had to say, and from time to time someone would ask me questions like "What is this dog saying? I think it is sad and needs healing. Will you ask it and tell us?" Then during the dolphin swim someone very interested in my book was asking excitedly "What are they saying? Tell me what the dolphins are saying now?" I replied that I had no idea what they were saying, just as I had explained that I could not link up with the dog. It was so hard to get over to people that I very seldom work in that way. When I am able to, I feel that there is some very special reason for it, or else that the angels have stepped in to help me because it is particularly important.

The workshop was officially over, and I wandered down to the beach contemplating a walk or a swim or both, when I saw one of the other participants sitting in a deck-chair in the shade. Something moved me to go and sit beside her. She appeared to be rather upset or bothered about something. "Can you hear the dolphin calls? I am hearing them all the time I am sitting here?" The last part was just as much a question as the first sentence I felt. I stopped to listen for a moment, but heard nothing. I realised that she meant that she was hearing them clairaudiently, as there was certainly nothing to hear with one's physical ears, and I could not hear them by any method. I did sense that there was certainly something going on, and I wanted to know if they were really with her or not. I spontaneously started to look clairvoyantly, and I saw about six dolphins in a vertical position surrounding her. Whilst seeking to answer my own questions, I found myself channelling a short personal message for her concerning what was coming from the dolphins. I found this so easy, as it seems to be what I am cut out to do. Another person might have done it better, but this way of working is what I really feel comfortable with. After I had finished the channelling, I too began to hear the dolphin calls clairaudiently.

Chapter 14

Dolphins and Inter-species Communication

"Do I share this life-time in my book?" I asked myself, "or do I just extract one or two little bits about dolphins, and omit the rest of it? Should I put all of it in?" "YES!!" came loud and clear from my inspirers, so that I could no longer doubt the wisdom of it. "Well," I told myself, "I enjoyed it so much when I recalled it in my (Light Institute) Session that it is possible others might also enjoy the adventure, whether they find it credible or not."

These were my thoughts about an E.T. life remembered and carefully recorded during one of my sessions in Chris Griscom's "Dolphin and Inter-Species Communication Workshop" which took place on an island near Belize in May of 1994.

Apart from Planet Earth which I visited during this time, I was unable to channel any names for the different places I visited, so I called the planet where I was born "Base Planet". Earth as number one keeps its own name in my story, and the rest I have numbered from two to six, and then invented my own names for them in the interests of clarity.

I reconnected with those beings in those long ago times (time is an illusion of course, but if it were not an illusion, then I would say that it all took place a very long time ago) in an unlikely way. I found myself as a fish, perhaps about twelve inches long swimming around in the depths of the ocean on Planet Earth. I began to experience how it was to be a fish. I drew my oxygen from out of the water, and had the ability too make quick and sudden movements, whereas when feeding I could feel the whole of my body quivering, as this was how I held myself still in the water. I had very good eyesight, and could see the bubbles in the water around me. As my eyes stuck out from my body, it was easy to see in all directions. Especially useful for keeping myself safe in dark places was something in my body that worked rather like radar. It was something that I could put out that would bounce back from the rocks or other life forms giving me warning of danger. I was able to negotiate my way safely through dark crevices where my eyes could no longer guide me. I was able to sense the consistency of what ever was in my environment, whether it was solid, inanimate, or the body of another fish. I could pick up signals from other fish and life-forms.

Having familiarised myself with how it was to be a fish, I began to look out through the fish's eyes and observe some very interesting goings-on in my environment. I saw beings with light bodies, almost on a different dimension, and obviously with no need to take in oxygen or air. They did not breath, and were living on the ocean floor. I could see myself swimming around them, but knew that I would not try to swim through them. I and my kind have an agreement with them to allow them their space. I saw that they were very connected to beings from outer space with whom they were related. These beings were doing research work. They had large computer-like brains in which they were able to store any information that they gleaned. They were studying the vibrations of the planet which were particularly clear on the ocean floor. They were feeling what was going on inside the planet. These extraterrestrial beings are living in a deep and remote part of the ocean where they are undisturbed by the activities of humans.

Next came the moment when I saw myself being eaten by a fish larger than myself. It appeared to be some kind of shark. It was a painless death as I released my consciousness allowing it to dwell temporarily with that of the shark who had swallowed me. It seemed as though for a few moments before I drifted away, I was the larger fish. On parting with it certain "knowings" came to me. First that being eaten just then was a necessary part of my plan. It was a timely, effective and convenient way of leaving that dimension having first found out what I needed to know about fish life. Secondly, that only a part of my consciousness had incarnated in that little fish, and that a larger part of it had remained in the living body of one of the E.Ts. that I had just been observing.

As visitors to the planet, we (the E.Ts.) wanted to know how it was for the sea life having us down there. The best way to find out was for one of us to incarnate as a fish. To be this little fish, it had only been necessary to release a small part of my consciousness, which could afterwards return to me in my light body, so I did not have to die in order to become a fish. This experience had taught me that if the fishes came too close to us, the vibrations were not compatible. For them it was like getting an electric shock if they came too close. Therefore it was important to communicate to the sea life that we did not wish to harm them, but that they must learn to keep their distance, otherwise they would be harmed.

We were visiting Planet Earth from our Base Planet. We were in frequent communication with the sea life, and also with each other. Therefore we had permanent lines of communication which were like shafts of light that we kept open for relaying messages and information back to our base on Base Planet. Not only could telepathic messages be sent down these shafts of light, but they could also be used as an entrance or exit to Planet Earth.

I found myself further back in time on Base Planet before my visits to Planet Earth. My body still looked like a light body with very high energy. To Earth people it would have looked transparent. It seemed to be full of electricity. It had a head, arms, legs, and body, but not in human form. Whereas the legs were much the same width all the way down, the trunk of the body was very little wider than an arm or a leg. Its contours were more angular then those of a human, more square or rectangular looking.

The Planet itself was an amazing place. Humans would not have survived there. This was partly because it was very radioactive, but as we understood that this radio-activity could be harmful for Planet Earth, we passed through a place like an energy area which removed the radio-activity from our systems, and yet left us with enough energy to operate each time before we visited Earth.

This cleansing had the effect of changing our vibrations very slightly, which diminished the length of time that we could safely remain away from home, and was one of the reasons why the energy lines for travel and communication had to be perfectly maintained all the while. In the early days three of us (but not me) had died in the ocean. This had been caused by staying on Planet Earth for too long at a time without any means of re-fuelling. So these beings lost their power that gave them their light, and I saw them as crumpled heaps of dark grey matter dispersing at the bottom of the ocean, and turning to dust. On our return home to Base Planet we passed through a large area of bright orange energy in order to recondition ourselves for our own Planet.

In our way we were very spiritual beings, and certainly not destructive. We had a close affinity with the element of fire which was just as well on Base Planet as there the energies moved a great deal, and the planet was very explosive. We needed to be able to feel when the next explosions would occur, so for our safety, we had learnt to tune into and communicate with the core essence of our planet by feeling the vibrations beneath us, that is the planet floor. Our planet was very wise, and had its own consciousness and spirit, which we sometimes perceived in a fiery form. It was the spirit of our own planet that first guided us to Earth. It told us that there was fire there, even beneath the waters. We went to Earth to communicate with it and Planet Earth told us:

"I am an evolving planet, and I am very rich in the variety of different elements that I hold. I have a multitude of different life-forms living and evolving with me, and part of my purpose is to stimulate these life-forms into growth of all kinds, into physical and spiritual evolvement. I do this by periodically changing the environment for them, thus presenting them with new challenges. Sometimes as I carry so much it feels hard to breathe, and then I need to tune into the power of my centre and with effort make the next move to free myself."

That is what the Earth said.

The spirit of Base Planet had knowledge of many other planets, and was so full of wisdom that we respected it like a god. It cared for us and our well-being. When we made journeys out to other planets, we were always guided by our own planet's spirit. It could advise us on the nature of our destinations and their whereabouts before we ever saw them. We ourselves also held much wisdom, for we had learned to listen to the other forms of consciousness around us. In addition, we had the desire to teach.

Planet Two, "The Malfunctioning Planet"

When we visited this planet, our main function was the passing on of our wisdom. The inhabitants there were living out of harmony with each other, and also with their planet, which itself was adversely affected. We found there a rapidly diminishing population who were not easy to help, as listening and tuning in to other beings and their surroundings was not part of their nature. They were not equipped with the necessary organs in their bodies to manage this without help. Therefore we constructed energy machines which they could use for this. They asked for our continued presence on their planet, as to them we were like a life-support machine. Thus their planet was saved from disaster.

The vibrations there were different from those of the Earth, and different from those on our planet. Therefore when leaving to visit the Malfunctioning Planet, we passed through a green energy field to adapt ourselves to it, and on our return through an energy field of orange and light, so that we would feel comfortable at home.

"Base Planet"

We loved our home very dearly. We were a loving and caring people, yet close physical contact was not part of our culture. We ourselves had no sex, but we were interested in the sexuality of other life-forms. Without sex, how did we manage to incarnate there? It happened like this. There was a place on Base Planet with a large square hole. Something that looked like orange flames came up out of it, but this was not fire, but another form of energy. When spirit forms wanted to incarnate here, they first had to connect with our consciousness, and only if they were successful in managing to do this did we gather round the hole in the ground and put out our energy, so that a body for the newcomer would be formed in the hole, and then this newly incarnated being would rise up from out of the flames in the hole to greet us.

When it came to death, some of us would die in the same way as the beings I had seen die in the bottom of the ocean on Planet Earth, but for those who consciously chose death it was different. We would gather around them in a special place where there were pale gold spirals of energy. The departing being would move into the energy spirals which then took up the substance of the body returning it to the planet, thus freeing the spirit to leave.

I lived for many years (in Earth time). There was plenty to do. There was learning that could be done on our own planet, as well as work on at least six other planets that I visited. Before any of these visits, there was always a telepathic communication with the planet to be visited asking for permission for our presence there, and we were guided both by the spirit of the distant planet and the spirit of our home planet in the adjustment of our vibrations for the visit.

Planet Earth Again

During that life-time, I only allowed part of my consciousness to incarnate as a fish once, but when I saw a rather larger and very beautiful sea creature swimming around, I approached this being, and sought permission to merge with its consciousness in order to learn and experience it from the inside. It was a dolphin. The consciousness of this large mammal was greatly expanded. It was like a brother to us, and I experienced great joy. The swimming and playing in the water were especially blissful. It was the most wonderful way in which to experience the element of water, something that we did not have at home. In other ways too it was a very enriching experience, for we learnt love and compassion more deeply than we had anywhere else. It was not unusual to do this, for I saw many of my fellow beings join consciousness with them. It was a very strong connection.

We also learnt other things from them. They helped us in our research, because they were so sensitive that they knew a great deal about what was happening in and around the Earth, and they thought of us as their brothers from the sky. We saw that many of these creatures (dolphins) were simultaneously living E.T. lives, and some of them also understood the human consciousness. I learnt from the dolphins that there was some kind of karmic connection between dolphins and humans. They called humans "the blind ones", because they could not perceive the dolphins as they were. The dolphins were waiting for the right opportunities to help heal the humans, to help them expand. They also called them "the sleeping ones".

Going way back in evolution there was a time when the dolphin and human consciousness was not yet divided. The dolphins still remembered it, but said that most humans had forgotten. The cause of the division was the need of consciousness to experience separation. It was like a sacrifice, which was made in order to obtain increased wisdom and understanding at the end. The dolphins had always held this memory in their hearts, almost as though we were their children.

(After these sessions were over, I learnt from Chris Griscom that the embryo or foetus of a baby dolphin is very similar to that of a human, with exactly the same bones and joints as we have, but then the development changes as it grows and takes the form of a dolphin.)

In this life as an E.T. some of my experiences on Planet Earth were the most moving that I had ever had. For example, experiencing emotion through the dolphin, because although we had emotions of a kind of our own they were not like human emotions which are very deep. I never did connect with human consciousness and emotion. During that particular experience, that period of time, we were more interested in creatures of the ocean, than of the land. We did not encounter them, and most of the time kept away from the shore. In my visions, however, I saw that the humans were receiving assistance from other E.Ts. That was not part of our purpose.

The nearest I came to encountering humans was this. Although it was very unusual for us to be on the land, on one occasion several of us visited a place with many rocks on the shore very close to the ocean, having been attracted by the vibrations there. We found ourselves looking at other visiting E.Ts., but not from our planet. These looked like little green men. They seemed to be existing in the rocks, some of which had salt water pools. We were able to communicate with them, and asked them what they were doing. They replied, "We came from another planet. We were not happy at home. We are choosing to try and live on Planet Earth." They went on to explain that they were not very happy about the humans here. There was mistrust, mostly on the part of the humans, and "When the humans are afraid, they attack. Therefore we hide," they explained. Very occasionally they had managed to make friends with one or two of the human children, but they could not be of service to each other apart from exchanging information. The little green men told us what they knew about humans, and we understood better what the dolphins meant, for they too had told us a few things concerning the humans, and we felt that the human race was not for us. We chose to return to the water. I had a great love for it. It was a wonderful element!

Planet Three, "The Reptiles' Planet"

There was one planet that we visited which was covered with animals like reptiles. This planet also had water, but with different vibrations and consistency than that of Planet Earth. The Reptiles' Planet had a green aura, and the consciousness of the reptile-like creatures was linked with the reptiles on Earth. The reptiles' consciousness existed on both planets by choice, as they wanted physical form, and by occupying both planets this was more sure. On the Reptiles' Planet, there still existed forms that have long been extinct on Planet Earth. When we worked there, our purpose was to help maintain the communication lines between the consciousness of those reptiles, and the consciousness of the ones on Planet Earth.

Planet Four, "The Recreational Planet"

I remembered another planet that we used to visit, which was populated by E.Ts. who were of a different culture. These beings were very flexible, and lived on a planet with rocks. When they chose to, they could just move the whole of their body and consciousness into the rock, and appear not to be there. There were plants on this planet, and the beings could merge with them also, and then walk out again intact. I found that wonderful! So wonderful! One moment I appeared to be alone on the landscape, and the next moment an E.T. would step out of a plant or rock as though appearing from nowhere. They did this deliberately, because they knew it pleased us to watch their magic. They said that they would be willing to teach us to do all this, but our bodies were not suitable for it. It was a very good friendship, and there was laughter on that planet. They took their nourishment by blending in this way with the rocks and the ground. The plants were like big juicy cacti.

The bodies of the E.Ts. were a dark red colour, but this colour disappeared altogether when they blended with a plant. We offered to help them with communication and travel. When we demonstrated, they watched us with great delight, but felt that they were not adjusted for travel, so we just enjoyed each other. For us this was like a recreational planet, thus the name I have given it, and it was there for the mutual enjoyment of its inhabitants and ourselves. In addition to sharing our knowledge with them, we also brought the gift of light in return for their hospitality.

When the Great Spirit of Base Planet informed us that E.T. raiders were heading for Recreational Planet, we took immediate action.

Planet Five, "The Partially Darkened Planet of the Red Raiders"

A large army of our people set out on light-rays to build up an energy shield to protect the Recreational Planet. It effectively made Recreational Planet invisible. Our mission was successful. When the Raiders hit the energy shield, it altered their course, and they just went skimming straight past the planet in their reddish coloured space ships. It seemed like the beginning of a star war. The Red Raiders came from a planet from outside our galaxy which was deficient in light, which is why I have called it "The Partially Darkened Planet".

Planet Six, "Beings of Light Planet"

We decided to alert some friends on the Beings of Light Planet to help us with this situation. These friends were strongly connected with the angelic realms, and it was decided to make combined efforts to flood the Partially Darkened Planet of the Red Raiders with light in order to raise their level of consciousness, and to help restore harmony and peace to the heavens. When I looked at the Partially Darkened Planet, I saw it as dark red, and misty grey with very little light.

(At this point in my session a little dog and a cat came along to tell me that it was time to move out of this lifetime, so I reluctantly informed my facilitator that we needed to finish, although it was not what I wanted, as I was really enjoying myself recalling these things. Therefore I moved on through time to see how I left Base Planet.)

I saw myself in the pale gold energy spirals on Base Planet. As I stood there, my body was taken back into the substance of the planet as my spirit ascended upwards into the light. This was an ecstatic experience, activating all of my bliss centres. The light was beautiful. It sparkled and filled my being. I had a resting time there, and then I moved into a realm where I had many friends for a joyous reunion.

Then the little dog and cat (who were nothing to do with Base Planet etc., but were present in spirit like guides for me) moved away which told me that things had taken place as they had intended them to.

I feel that it is appropriate to complete this chapter with a brief account of events in 1995 which have helped me with these last two chapters as I promised I would "in a later chapter" when I was half way through chapter 13.

Knowing that the summer would be too full and busy for much writing, I carefully finished chapter 13 in April. The book was laid aside, and I made no attempt to come back to it before November. Meanwhile my first book had come out in Spanish. At the end of October I had spent two weeks in Israel swimming with dolphins, and on my return home to a large pile of mail, the very first letter that I picked up, opened and read was from Sergi Ayno, a dolphin-loving Spaniard who had just read my book, and wanted to share his thoughts with me. He told me how he led workshops, sessions and lectures about connecting with dolphins. Even this tiny little bit of information made me realise that I had left out most of the good bits in chapter 13, mostly because I thought that I had no proof that my work was valid, and no one would believe it. Discovering that someone like Sergi was being attracted to my books and taking the contents seriously gave me the confidence to rewrite the chapter, and this time I put all the good bits in.

The next event was a second letter from Sergi. In my response to his letter, I had referred very briefly to my dolphin encounters when I was an E.T. mentioned already in this chapter. Imagine my excitement when I read the second letter in which he told me how he had recalled his own dolphin life where his mission had been to be like a bridge between human-beings and extraterrestrial brothers and sisters. In both letters he referred to the existence of a city of light in the depths of the ocean, which seemed to confirm the reality of my E.T. existence on the sea floor, just as I have described it.

My heart leapt with joy. It was just the revelation that I needed.

Later, in February of 1996, I met Sergi Ayno, first in London, and then in Barcelona where I had gone to give a talk on my first book.

The last day of my short visit was a holiday, so Sergi and I spent a lot of time together. The important outcome of our meeting was that neither of us have any doubts now that Sergi was the dolphin whose consciousness I had the privilege of sharing in the E.T. life that I have just described.

Chapter 15

Beings Who Live in the Earth

I knew nothing of these Beings. I had neither read about them, or heard about them, so the whole experience was a complete surprise to me.

I had recently enjoyed several interesting trips to other planets during my meditations, and my guides were well aware that I appreciated the adventure. Several times now I had simply lifted off the Earth in the company of at least one angel-like being, and had allowed myself to be taken to what ever interesting venue the angel guides had had in mind for me. This only happened when I had a willing escort. Other times, disappointed, I had to stay at home.

On 18th. March, 1989, as I sat down on the pink carpet in my own house to meditate, I sensed that something interesting was about to take place. It did not start in the usual way. Instead I was shown a very strong-looking belt. It was quite big, so although it was securely fastened, it was possible for me to step into it. As I placed it around my waist, it shrank to a perfect fit. It had a strong chain attached to it, which I felt was as long as necessary, and very elastic. This chain would act like a silver cord, and keep me connected to Earth no matter how far I went. My guides, two in number, chose to remain invisible, but I was able to sense their presence, and for a brief moment, I felt hands on my body supporting me and lifting me as I left the room (mental body only).

I travelled very swiftly, still confident that the unseen guides were with me. I had been hoping that this would be a trip to Venus, because surely we would be visiting another planet. Therefore I was rather surprised when I found myself approaching somewhere that looked very similar to the Earth. At the time I assumed that this was another planet, but one that looked like Earth. I saw something like snow lying on much of the ground, and a pleasantly undulating landscape with many pine trees. My attention was drawn to a very small mountain or hill formed rather like a cone-shaped sea shell with sloping sides and not very tall. I ascended its ridges, and on reaching the summit, without knowing why, I started to rub the highest part which was violet-coloured and shiny. The rest of the mountain was shades of sand and coral, the colours of winter grasses. To my amazement, the small violet dome disappeared, and a tiny black hole grew larger forming an entrance with a purple rim around it that led into the mountain.

Whatever force it was that had powered and piloted my journey so far took my spirit onward through this opening, at first dimly lit, but as I travelled on it soon became a black dark tunnel. With no angels or guides in sight, I felt very glad of the belt around my waist, and the feeling that in the event of any danger I could be pulled all the way back to the place I had come from by the chain attached to it. It was the belt and chain that gave me the courage to keep going in the dark without any knowledge of where or what I was moving towards. After a while I saw a faint glimmer of purple light ahead, and then deep blues and lilac and pale blue and some white. The tunnel broadened out at the end rather like a rabbit warren, and there were these Beings, nine or ten of them gathered together in a rough circle. It seemed natural not to greet them with a hug, but by walking round them sliding my hand down the back of each in turn, which was followed by a similar greeting for me from each of them.

These "people" seemed to be living in etheric bodies rather than being fully physical. They were slightly transparent, whereas the rest of the environment appeared solid. Communicating with telepathy, I asked them if they always lived underground. "No," they replied, "sometimes we go out for fresh air and light, and to enjoy our beautiful planet." Immediately I was taken on a guided tour of 'above ground' by them. Instead of leaving their underground cavern through the tunnel I had come through, we took another one. It was lighter, had soft shades of green, and sloped gently upwards. As we emerged from the interior of the mountain, we did not walk, but sped over the ground horizontally (like low flying aircraft). I had several Beings on either side of me, for once out of the tunnel, we travelled abreast. We flew through the dark green pine trees, to a beautiful pale green area (grass I would think) and back again into the mountain. I had seen no other signs of civilisation, only Nature.

Re-assembled in their cavern, I wanted to know how their bodies were nourished. They said that they could obtain much of what they needed directly from the atmosphere, but they also showed me water dripping through the rocks. This water was an interesting shade of red, and they said that it was rich in minerals which seeped down from the earth above. They are replenished by Nature. "We leave her undisturbed," they said, "so that she is able to keep herself in perfect balance. It works better when we do not interfere."

"Why do you live underground?"

"Because we want the Earth to stay beautiful. Living underground, we barely disturb her. Nature is free to balance herself. There are plenty of beautiful roots growing in the forest, and taking one or two on special occasions does not spoil the forest, but these are not necessary for us to live."

"How long do you stay here?"

"Most of us live here for about two or three hundred years."

"Why do you stay for so long?"

"Because we can evolve here. We do not stay the same. We are always changing, therefore it is not necessary to go and live on other planets, or change our bodies more often." (They meant re-incarnate.)

"How do you reproduce?"

"New people do not come very often, but when they do, they come drifting in in embryo-form, and are able to draw enough substance to themselves to form bodies like ours. We help nourish them in our groups. Your type of pregnancy is not necessary for us, because we are not so physical any more."

"What makes the light down here?"

They showed me something like a large crystal on the ceiling which could be gently rubbed with one's hand, and then it gave out white light. I saw several of these dotted around.

"What replenishes the crystal?" I wanted to know.

"It is connected through the rocks to the surface, and draws light in from there."

It was not a very bright light, but I guess it was enough for them. All of this communication had been telepathic. Any time one of my questions was not answered, I simply repeated the question, and then the answer came, but mostly asking once was sufficient.

At last I felt that I had obtained enough information, and it was time to go home. I explained this to them, and said goodbye. At first when I started to make a written record of this afterwards, I thought I had forgotten to thank them, but then more pictures came back to me. It was like this.

I very gently exhaled a soft golden light into the middle of their circle. I felt that I was channelling this light from a distant planet, where I felt that the energies were pure. I was not sure how people living in these semi-dark conditions would receive this light. Thus the gentleness of my exhalation, but they seemed to be happy with it.

I felt myself being pulled very swiftly backwards down the dark tunnel of my first entry, and with lightning speed back to my home. I thanked my guides for the experience, and they made it clear (I think that it was by showing me a pen) that I should write it all down. I did.

For the following six months, I was perfectly happy believing that this had all taken place on another planet, which was clearly of the same density as Planet Earth, and with many similarities. Then I went to Switzerland for a week, and met a French lady. She listened with great interest and attention to the above story, and then said, "Yes, I know about these people, but they are not on another planet, they are living underground on Planet Earth."

Four years later in March of 1993, Linda Tellington-Jones gave me a copy of "The Prism of Lyra". In this book I found plenty of information in chapter nine about galactic beings called the "Zeta Reticuli" which gave me ample grounds to accept that the Beings I had met did exist, and furthermore, that they had chosen to live here on Planet Earth.

About a month after that, when I made a brief connection with the Ascended Masters, one of them showed me the head and shoulders of one of the Reticuli. The head was egg-shaped, and the eyes large with dilated pupils to fill the whole of the eye. There was a glow of blueish purple light coming from the eyes which I understood aided vision. Apart from the eyes, all was a ghostly white, that is, not fully opaque.

This led me to refer to the book again where I had seen an illustration, and I found that it matched very well with what I had been shown. The author describes how the eyes have evolved in this way to assist vision in very poor light.

In my meditation in 1989, I never had a clear view of the face of any one of them, so I cannot say if their eyes were like this or not. However, they always responded to me like a single being, as one consciousness, and this I have since read is one of the characteristics of the Zeta Reticuli. I believe that there are several different strains of them, but that they are not all resident here, and that I was guided to those who wished only good for me.

Chapter 16

Elephants

This information seemed to come almost as an answer to the questions that I had had in my mind about elephants. Since the animals started to communicate with me, I had begun to watch wild-life documentaries on the television, something that I had never really shown interest in before. I found them very intriguing, but it bothered me that I had once channelled a poem (included in my first book) called "*The Song of the Elephants*." which begins,

> "*The wisdom that we bring*
> *See the wisdom that we bring*".

Yet the T.V. documentaries showed us how destructive they were, how they demolished the trees, stole the supplies of the local farmers, and behind them left a barren desert. The planet is so short of trees, therefore I could see little wisdom in the behaviour of the elephants.

So on 23rd. March, 1994, in my meditation at home, the elephants spoke to me.

"It is survival. Life for us on planet Earth is about survival at this present time. We behave as we do in conditions where only one tree remains, but we need food, so we destroy the last tree in the desert. We take from the farmers as all that we understand is that we need the food that they have to survive."

I understood.

Next I found myself swept away from these scenes on the Earth, and taken to another planet. I saw families of elephants walking peacefully through an abundant growth of trees. It was obvious that on this other planet nourishment was in such an abundance that they did not have to struggle to survive. It was shown to me how without the survival struggle, they were free to evolve in different ways to the elephants on planet Earth. I saw the love and the caring amongst the family groups, (also the case on Earth very often I believe,) and I also saw that they were full of wisdom. They were very special on this distant planet, even when compared with the other beings there. The elephants were the carriers of wisdom, for they held much of it in their beautiful dome-shaped heads. It was even visible, for it was as a light that they carried. It made them look just as though someone had inserted a light bulb in the centre of each of the brains of the adults, which then glowed gently through the elephants' thick skin. In the young ones the light was weaker, but growing.

As they finished descending a gentle slope they reached a small clearing, where they were greeted by the resident E.Ts.. These beings were two legged as we are, but they were less solid, carried more light, and had lovely gentle and fine vibrations. They recognised the wisdom of the elephants, and they had an agreement that when they needed wisdom for themselves to help them continue to exist in a harmonious way with their planet, by touching the forehead of one of the oldest and wisest elephants, some of this wisdom was transferred to them, although the elephant did not lose it.

As I looked around to get a better understanding of the nature of this planet, I had the feeling that it was situated somewhere on the very edge of the universe. It was very old. Even the trees were of a great age, for I could see how aged and worn the trunks of some of them were. However the planet was far far older than its trees, and much older than Planet Earth. At its beginning, it had been just as physical and solid as our planet, but now I could see space between the particles that formed its density. It was held together by the collective thought power of those who still wanted it there, as though its natural gravity had worn out eons of time ago. It was peacefully suspended in a very special place. Had it

116

been anywhere else in the universe, it would most probably have been blown apart, or shattered by meteorites hurtling through space. The energies round this planet were very still. There was some movement, but only like the gentlest of breezes compared with other places. It was like an isolated patch of still water in a mighty ocean called the universe. I watched the particles of energy around it. Sometimes they appeared like grains of sand, where each one was a different colour, and each particle shone with its own light. It was a veritable paradise. I felt that it would continue to exist in this way for as much longer as it was needed. It gave balance to the Universe. It held the energies of peace and harmony, while there is chaos and violence and disruption in other places. I tried to get an idea of its size, although I knew that this was intellectual curiosity, and not of importance. I felt that it might be larger than the Earth, but only a little, and that neither of these two planets is really of any great size.

This felt like a story that had been arrested before the end, as there was so much more that I would like to have seen of this place, but thirty minutes had passed which was the agreed length of time for meditating that night with my friend, so I dared to assume that if I was intended to know more it would be shown to me at a later date.

Since then, although no further information has been given to me, I have found that I only have to think briefly about it, and I feel so connected to the wonderful spiritual peace that I experienced there, that it is like healing for the soul.

Chapter 17

Mainly Trees

On October 8th. and 9th. (1994) I stayed in Chedworth for a weekend seminar called "Communication with Animals." After driving down there late the preceding evening at the end of a very busy week, I felt too tired to walk straight into lectures at 10 a.m. prompt on Saturday morning, so as my soul was yearning for the pleasures of nature, fresh air, and the feel of the beautiful autumn sunshine, I set off on foot to enjoy a mixture of footpaths, bridleways and quiet country lanes. These included a track through some ancient woodland, where I felt moved to stop, and communicate with a very old enormous oak tree.

My arms were far too short to reach more than a little way around its trunk, but I stood there with my body close against it, my forehead resting on the aged bark, and tuned myself in.

I perceived the spirit of the tree to look like a little old man sitting inside it. "I knew that you were coming." he said. I asked if there was anything that he would like to communicate to me, or show me. There was a question in my mind concerning how humanity would ever manage the transition into a state of raised consciousness and the quickened vibrations that are thought to be necessary for the changes taking place on this planet relatively shortly. "We will help you. The trees will help mankind." answered the tree. At this point we moved into a world of pictures, feelings, and sounds.

I felt the tree just being there. It was a rich existence. There was the music of the stream running past close beside it, there was the bird song, all the noises from the various lifeforms in the forest, and the wind rustling in the trees, with the sound of trees swaying in the wind. There was the music of the cosmos, that something in the atmosphere inaudible to physical ears, but which can be perceived as a certain vastness stretching forever giving a wonderful sense of space and expansion. Closer at hand, the tree showed me pictures of the energies rising and falling within itself, and the dimension of the nature spirits. The atmosphere took on a mystical appearance with so many sparkling lights, and so much vibrant life-force. I could not say where the tree ended, and another tree or a blade of grass began. I saw how the life-forms did not have clearly defined borders around their auras as I would have expected, but instead they all seemed to blend into one another. Here the tree spirit explained a bit.

"We are all part of the same whole. We know that. We blend with one another, and have not specialised in individualization in the way that humanity has, leading them to believe that they are all separate entities even from each other. This connectedness enables us to know what is happening far far away. To live in one place is therefore the same as existing in many places simultaneously."

I found myself musing on the inter-dependency of the different life forms, as it came into my mind how many different little creatures were dependent on the oak, perhaps nibbling away at its leaves.

I felt that I had just received my spiritual nourishment for the morning, and as my inner voice was calling me to move on, I thanked the tree, and sent it love in the form of light before I left, and went to join everyone else at the seminar.

The seminar was wonderful. There were two speakers, Kate Solisti, and Shelley Donelley. On the second day, when I managed to attend all of it (I think), one of the speakers told us how the boundaries between other life forms are not as clearly defined as ours, but blend into each other more, and the other kingdoms have not specialised in individualization in the same way that we have.

Secondly, while I was sitting there listening to what was being said, I saw an eagle flying towards me. It took hold of me by the scruff of the neck, and in a picture, I saw myself being put down at the front close to the speakers. I felt that the eagle came from the Council of Animals, and that it wanted me to talk to Kate Solisti after she had finished her lecture and demonstration, so I did. It seems that she also sees mermaids, "popping up all over the place rather like fairies." She told me that mermaids were something out of a bygone age, as were unicorns (my brief encounter with a unicorn is described in my first book) and dragons. I valued this confirmation very highly, especially coming from a psychic communicator who did it all in such a natural way, and for whose work I have great respect.

The second speaker, Shelley Donelley, spoke freely and quite extensively about a "Council of Animals"! Hearing the existence and nature of the Council of Animals being openly discussed in front of an audience of this size also had a very profound effect on me. I felt encouraged, and more confident.

On 6th. October 1995, being a keen hiker, I set out rather late in the afternoon to explore some of the beautiful hill country near Llangollen in Wales. I was enjoying myself too much to plan my route so that I would be back at the car park in the daylight, so the last couple of hours were spent in the dark following an "easy to find" very narrow deserted lane back to Llangollen. I was enjoying the stillness of the night, the sound of a little brook running over the rocks, the company of a cat who interrupted its nocturnal hunting expedition to come to me for a little attention, and the freshness of the air, when I found myself attracted to a particularly large tree. I had already looked longingly at some of the other sizable trees, but this one, I felt, was special.

When people are around, I am too self-conscious to feel comfortable about standing there with my body pressed up against a tree, and my arms stretched as far around its trunk as they can reach with my eyes closed, and apparently doing nothing! By this time, however, it was raining gently as well as dark, so the likelihood of anyone else walking down the lane for pleasure was remote. Therefore I decided that the odds were heavily against my being discovered, so in the way I have just described, I made physical contact with the tree. I was not trying to get a message. I just wanted to be with it, and feel it. Unexpectedly, a part of my spirit or consciousness slipped into the tree. It was as though the tree had taken me, or drawn me into itself. I felt one with the tree, and as I looked around from inside it, there were these beautiful bands of rainbow colours all around it. I enjoyed this for a little while, thanked the tree, and then I left.

This is a beautiful example of enjoying Nature just by allowing oneself to be one with it. Dialogue is not necessary to make the connection meaningful.

Chapter 18

Animal Lives and Other Life-forms

This chapter is a collection of separate experiences of several people including me, all of them in some way illustrating the chapter title.

Although I knew roughly what the subject matter for this chapter was to be, I had a plan not to write it just yet, but to take a pause from writing while I learnt a little Spanish, which would be useful for my trip to Barcelona where I was destined to give a talk (in English) about my first book.

Meanwhile, I decided to arrange a massage for myself during a planned visit to London, but when I tried to arrange it, the lady was away, and therefore I spoke to her secretary/partner. Alex knows me quite well, so we started a friendly chat, and I was more than a little surprised when in spite of knowing nothing about the title of this chapter, and with no prompting from me, completely spontaneously, Alex started to tell me about two of her own past lives, one as a cat, and one as a large brown/black bear. To me this was just as uncanny and remarkable as Sergi Ayno's letters arriving just as I was writing about dolphins had been. I took it as a hint from the Universe that the chapter needed to be written immediately, and hoped, as I lay my Spanish text book aside, that the Spaniards were better at English than I am at Spanish. This is a controversial subject (like the rest of my book!), and the possibility that any humans have ever been incarnated as animals is rejected by many. It went through my mind, however, that the more people who got as far as thinking that this might be possible, the better would be the fate of the animals living on

Planet Earth. I felt that even if the possibility of it happening was very remote, that it could not be proven to be impossible. Perhaps with this belief we would become more like the practising Buddhists who have great reverence and respect for all life.

Alex remembered two types of experience. In the first one, she recalled flying with an eagle. She was not the eagle, she knew that, but was allowed to be carried by the consciousness of that bird as though she were an eagle. This is what I call 'shared consciousness', when one is allowed the privilege of experiencing being the other being, and feeling how that is, but not controlling it, even though one may never have been incarnated in that form personally.

I have had this type of experience on a number of occasions. For example, with a fish which I mentioned in my first book (though that may have been a past life. I was never completely sure), and quite definitely with a dolphin as I have described in Chapter 14 of this book.

Alex's second type of experience was the two 'other' lives. As the first of these was recalled, she wondered what she could be doing with her nose so close to the paving stones. Then she realised that she was a cat, and noticed how some of the people (they must have seemed enormous) bent down to stroke her, while others did not like her, and tried to kick her out of the way. (It must have been a very insecure existence).

As a very large dark coloured brown/black bear, she had cubs, and they lived in a cave. Alex remembered how the entrance to the cave was very narrow, but just wide enough for her to be able to squeeze through it. When recalling this, she had been fascinated with the way in which she used her big paws. She was not able to say exactly how many cubs there had been, and this is precisely my experience when in a changed state of consciousness. It can be very hard, if not impossible sometimes, to do simple things like counting, even when all is there to see. (The beta, i.e. 'thinking' brain waves are often to some extent temporarily arrested, a good thing as in my opinion it helps with the purity of the information.)

Next I thought of Linda Tellington-Jones. Back in March of 1993, as I mentioned in chapter 4, I was in Germany with Linda, and, something I have not previously mentioned, I saw a dinosaur in her aura one night at dinner. Although I failed to write this down at the time, I remember the conversation going something like this:

"Linda! I know this sounds rather odd, but I can see a dinosaur in your aura."

"Really! Is it brown with a very small head, a very long neck, and a very long tail?"

"Yes. That's exactly what it looks like. How on Earth did you know what I was seeing?"

"Well, I had a past life as a dinosaur, and sometimes I still feel that I want to reach out and down with my long neck to graze the grass."

It was the very largest species of dinosaur. Linda quoted the latin name for it, which I managed to forget very quickly, as I sat there musing over what I had just seen and heard. That was the end of our dinosaur conversation.

I did not feel comfortable about publishing this story without Linda's permission, so knowing that this was one of the very rare times of the year when I might find her at home, I telephoned the States, and spoke to a very helpful Linda. With permission granted, the first point to add is that Linda has no way of knowing whether this was a past life or not. She may have assumed that it was, but really it is for each of us to draw our own conclusions. What Linda is sure about is how she experiences it. It seems that nearly every time that she takes her blue-green algae food supplement in the morning, she finds herself as this dinosaur standing in the marshes reaching down with that long dinosaur neck of hers to take large mouthfuls of blue-green algae, which (as 'Linda') she finds makes her laugh because it is so funny!

Another time, when Linda had not really started going into other lives, but was in a changed state of consciousness, and working with someone who was helping her have this experience, she discovered herself moving through water with a wonderful ease, and the most amazing joy you could imagine. At first she could not make out how this could be, as she was not aware of having any arms or legs. Then she realized that she was a dolphin, and living in the Mediterranean Ocean somewhere near Delphi in Greece she thought.

I was aware of a life as a monkey, but was never able to follow it up to get the details. I think that it did not matter. I have told of my experiences of life as a fish in chapter 14, and I have lost count of how many times other people have told me that they have had a life or even lives as a dolphin. Were these experiences real? Was it shared consciousness? Dare I add imagination to the list of possibilities? One could attempt to imagine these things, but for me it would not be real, as I would be limited to experiencing only the things that I could think of, whereas when it is real, one can have or relive experiences which certainly do not come from this lifetime. That is the magic of it.

While meditating at home on 31/10/'94, more information came my way. I found myself in a jungle with some elephants. One in particular was close to me, and I soon found myself on its back. Sitting there, I had the pleasure of being able to see the tops of the trees, and look at the birds who were sitting in them. I enjoyed the green lusciousness of the foliage, the being outside, and having such close contact with nature. The company of the elephants felt very pleasant. I felt at one with them.

The elephant I was sitting on took me at a smart trot through the trees until we reached a pool of clear water. This is where I slipped down from the elephant's back, and cleansed myself in the water. It was also the last I saw of the elephants that evening. They had completed their task.

The cleansing in the water was part of the usual cleansing ritual that I so often go through in meditation before receiving information, or having a deeper experience. It happened spontaneously, although the exact order of events after I stepped out of the water is hard to recall.

I was standing just behind a dinosaur. It was a greyish colour with a scaly skin. Its tail on the ground seemed to help to balance it. I was drawn closer into the picture, and felt my connections with this animal in the dinosaur age. I felt that once upon a time this had been me, so I tried to get a really good look at it as I wanted to know what sort of dinosaur I had been. It was not the long necked variety, but had quite a stubby looking shortish thick set neck, and a head with large jaws, and lots and lots of sharply pointed teeth. (At this point, my consciousness was experiencing this from the inside. I was being the animal. My jaws moved freely, and I seemed to enjoy gnashing my teeth at things. I am not quite sure what sort of diet I ate, but I felt that those teeth could have gnashed their way through nearly anything, and nothing was sacred. A mouthful of the nearest tree would do, and maybe meat as well. Most food was swallowed in fairly undigested lumps, that is, not well chewed up first.

This was the connection with that time on planet Earth that left me with the ability to connect with the spirit of these creatures, and is why I was easily able to be shown them by my inner child in the middle of one of my Light Institute sessions as I have related in Chapter 12. I vaguely perceived other creatures of those times around me, some of them in the air. The dinosaur that was me had no inhibitions. A certain fieriness in my dinosaur nature was readily expressed. I would never have thought of holding back my temperament. It was free flowing energy, no blocks. I felt a very natural way of being in that creature, almost dragon-like, and a deep and real way of experiencing life in the flesh.

My consciousness moved on, and I found myself connecting with mermaid energies again. It was clear to me that I had also been one of those on more than one occasion. (Others I have met have told me so have they.) This makes a natural opening through which the mermaid consciousness can connect with me now. I had the feeling that there was a lot about mermaids which I had not yet recalled. For the purpose of this meditation, it was shown to me that balancing on my tail in the body of a human is not a practical idea! I was given a large pair of scissors, and instructed to cut off the end of my tail which I did. Without a doubt this sounds bizarre, and is best not taken too literally, but I understood it to mean that unknown to me, I was still carrying around some facet of the mermaid reality or form which in some way inhibited me when in a human two-legged body, and removing the end of my tail was a symbolic way of freeing my feet for a more balanced existence as a homo sapien.

Next, I drifted into the world as it was when unicorns were incarnate. They had such a mystical energy about them. I saw both mermaids and unicorns as overlapping the human era, and also that the veil between the different realities was much thinner then. I found myself wondering if these beings and mermaids had

coincided with the Atlantean age. It was as though everyone was psychic. The energies of the environment, and the boundaries between the dimensions were less well defined, and many were aware of them. This knowledge, and these abilities where the human race was concerned were not always looked upon as an advantage. Fear of such things was rife, and so was abuse of power, a combination that led to the closing down of many people's psychic faculties, thus leading into a dark age of materialism and widespread ignorance of things beyond the dense physical reality. The more sensitive beings such as unicorns chose to leave the planet and continue their existence elsewhere.

Owls were another life-form that was brought to my attention. I felt that a certain rather shy form of E.T. consciousness was often incarnated in these birds, and that they chose to be birds of the night, as this was an effective method of keeping a distance between themselves and mankind. At the same time, it provided them with the opportunity to be here, and experience life in physical form. Thus ended my evening meditation.

The stories in this chapter are just a very few examples from diverse sources, whereas I feel sure it would be possible with more research to write a whole book on the subject.

Chapter 19

The Black Widow Spider

After the first day's sessions during the Feminine Fusion workshop in November 1991 with Chris Griscom's Light Institute in Galisteo, we gathered together after dinner in small groups to share what had happened during our one-to-one sessions.

I was asked if I would share first, but only a few words had escaped from my mouth before someone said to me in tones of alarm, "You have got something on you!" I looked, and crawling, or "running" is perhaps closer, I saw an unidentified black object hurrying across my lap. Luckily I was wearing trousers, so it was not on my skin. Nonetheless, I have always had a horror of small insects such as earwigs, for example, who can nip you, and therefore I flew into instant panic, and threw myself off my chair, hoping to escape from underneath it, but off course what ever it was hung on tight, so it was still with me. The person who had first seen it was by now organised enough to brush it off me with her paper folder, for which I was most grateful. As we watched it making its way across the floor, it was quickly identified by those native to the area as a black widow spider. "What would I have been like if I had known that when it was still on me?" I wondered to myself, as I had heard horrific tales of the effects of its very powerful and poisonous bite. It then started to make its way towards someone else at which point it was decided that it should be removed from the room. It was taken out alive, and no one was bitten.

I settled down, recovered my composure, and continued to share my session without any further disruptions. At the end of the evening when our little group was disbanding, I asked if such spiders often came into the house, and learnt that no, this was the first time. Then someone said, "You had better watch out tomorrow. If a black widow spider comes, it means that one of you is possessed! Who did it sit on anyway?" "Me." I reluctantly replied. Unfortunately I did not realise that this was supposed to be a lighthearted good-humoured joke. I took it completely seriously, and started worrying about it. Furthermore, it made me feel like an outcast.

First of all, I considered how illogical it was to believe that I was carrying any possessive energies at this particular time, as my sense of well being had been better than ever over the preceding few months. Also, I had had experience of possessive energies, and done much work to clear them from my person and send them to the Light, and through this experience had developed some skill in recognising their presence. I felt no such presence now. Nonetheless I wondered if some very subtle being was hiding itself so carefully in my auric field, that I was unable to detect it.

Just in case this was so, when I went for a walk the following morning, I did various clearing exercises with the use of white light, so that anything that was with me which should not have been would get the opportunity to return to the Light, and that any dark residues could be transmuted into light. At no point was I aware of any undesirable entities leaving me.

Just as a final touch, I decided to send the widow spider some love and light. I visualised the spider in order to make the contact, and then saw her surrounded with this soft pink colour, and lots of white light. Pink (colour of love), I felt, was the best colour for her.

Although I considered that I had done everything possible to look after myself, I still felt that it was right to tell my facilitator at the beginning of my next session what had happened, just in case she could help, or knew any more about the esoteric significance of black widow spiders than I did. We agreed that what I had done was more than adequate to clear anything that might have been there, although most probably it had not really been necessary, and the lesson for me appeared to be remembering that in such situations, I did not need to run to someone else for help, as I had enough power and intuitive knowledge of my own to deal

with them myself. The subject was then closed, and we went on to discuss other things, until the time arrived when I was about to get myself ready for the part of the session where we would work on clearing other lives.

Instead of rising from my comfortable chair immediately to prepare myself for the session, I hesitated, because I was starting to feel something very strange, something that I had never felt before in my life.

"Something is happening." I said to Yana, (my facilitator,) who was sitting directly opposite me. I began to sense a very powerful energy field that was now surrounding me. It seemed to fill most of the room, and I was sitting in the centre of it. I noticed with my inner eye that I could see the black widow spider sitting in a space just a little to my right and slightly above me.

The most interesting thing about this was, that she was still surrounded with the soft pink that I had sent her earlier in the day. A second strange thing was the way that she manifested herself with eyes that were large enough for me to know that she was looking at me. They were tinged with the same hue of soft pink that surrounded her. Also this time, she was there of her own will, for I had not attempted any contact. It came from her now.

As the energy field intensified, I told Yana that I had a black widow spider with me. When I had made it clear that the spider was on another dimension, and she understood that we did not need to evacuate the room, she asked me, "What does the spider want?" I passed the question on, and the answer came "To be accepted for being what we are." I understood the answer to be coming not from an individual spider, but from the group consciousness of the species. How normal and touching I found this. After all, is not this exactly what I had always wanted for myself? Just to be accepted as I am? Not to feel that I have to change, or behave in some other way before the people around me find me acceptable? All this made the spider's request seem so perfect and natural.

Meanwhile I was still experiencing this unique energy field. I spoke openly of it to Yana as it took place. It was almost overwhelming, and yet not quite. I felt no fear, but was totally fascinated by the novelty of this thing that I had never felt before in this lifetime. I kept my eyes open throughout. The energy field was so dense, that as I looked across to Yana, I saw her not clearly, but through a cloud. "I can still see." I thought to myself, "but I am looking through this brownish greyish mist that now surrounds me." I frequently repeated things like "Wow! I have never felt anything like this before!" I felt lost for words that could really describe it. In spite of the colour of the mist, I felt in no way threatened. I was comfortable in it, and it did not feel unfriendly or evil, just totally different. They really do seem to exist on another frequency, these spiders, but at least communication and understanding are possible.

After I had accepted the spider's reply, I saw her turn round and run away. I did not feel that she was in any particular hurry, but then spiders usually move quickly in my experience. At the same time, the energy field that she had brought was instantly lifted. It disappeared just as quickly as the spider left. I was sitting there in my chair still gasping with amazement at what had happened. Then Yana told me that it had also been a powerful experience for her. She had felt the changing energies in the room as well. I was truly grateful for her presence, as it really helps to validate these experiences when another person is able to confirm it, even if, as in this case, I am certain that the communication is real.

Later in the day, when still searching for any hidden meaning that might have escaped me, someone told me that sometimes when a particular animal visits one, it can be an omen of something coming. There was one way in which I could relate to this, and that was that in the following session, I re-experienced a life in which, as a female, I had grossly exploited and mis-used my feminine power; and the widow spider, I learnt, is apt to eat her mate after mating. The only difference is that in her case she is acting in accord with nature's proper cycle, whereas in my case, (though I omit the details here,) what I did was definitely not acceptable!

The following February I met Yana again, and she told me how it had been like an initiation for her. After this incident, the animals had started visiting her on a metaphysical level.

Experiencing the powerful energy field of the widow spider changed my own feelings towards the insect kingdom. It is hard to express it in words, but I feel that it would be fair to say that I recognised it, I felt a deeper respect for its presence, I wondered at it, and I realised that there was a far greater force behind it than I had ever previously suspected.

Chapter 20

A Very Busy Evening
With the Animals

When I get to the beginning of this, you may consider that I am choosing to start this story in a way that is not entirely fitting for a spiritual book, but if I dare to assume that all who read this have chosen to go through this life-time in a physical human body, then how I felt in the next paragraph could happen to you too!

I had reached a point during my meditation on 30th. January 1995, when I could sense that I was about to travel somewhere with my guides. There I was standing on my feet without clothes, as is normal for me on these trips, and aware of several angels around me. I felt uneasy in myself. It seemed to me that something was missing, and it was not my clothes. "There ought to be something between my legs" I thought silently to myself, as I remembered how I was missing having a man in my life at this time. I had forgotten that all of my thoughts are audible to those who live in other dimensions. "That's quite all right. We know what you want." came the unasked for reply from one of the angels. Somehow, having this desire (sexual urge) acknowledged enabled me to put it out of my mind for the rest of my meditation.

In Chapter 10 I spoke of the way in which the angels, or my guides often choose to cleanse me before taking me further in my meditational journeys. This is how they prepared me this time.

I saw a ray of light that appeared to lead to the sun, and knew that I was to travel up it. I saw a boat shaped upturned leaf for me to travel in. Its underside was furry and soft and comfortable.

I cannot say if the leaf was very large, or I had become very small, but either way, it was exactly the right size for me to travel in. I started travelling, but at this point I was having difficulty staying in the meditation, and it was as though I had become stuck. I shared this problem with one of the angels, who tied a piece of string around the stalk of the leaf, so that I was pulled up the ray of light, which was much easier. We did not go all the way to the sun, but after a certain distance, I disembarked, and stood in a place where I felt pretty sure that it was time for me to be cleaned up.

At first I seemed to be under a shower of silver-golden light particles, but then as that stopped, I noticed an angel standing behind me holding a shower-head, and directing its water at me with one hand, while cleaning me up with a good rub down with the other hand. When this was complete, we ascended a little higher on foot to a place where there was a lovely waterfall. The water was cascading down over a rock-face, and although at first I stood under the water, there was a little ledge behind it which I later stepped onto, and from where I could see how the vegetation growing around this place was a very bright green. In the middle of the rock ledge was a deep dark circular pool of clean water. I sank down into it feet first. I loved the darkness of it. As my body surfaced the helping hand of an angel was there to raise me up out of the water, but I chose to sink down into its black depths again, and this time stayed down there for longer, enjoying its restful peace, and the stilling effect that the darkness had on my mind. The second time that I surfaced, the angels made it quite clear that it was time to get out, as two of them hauled me up onto the rocky ledge. By this time, I must have been considered clean enough for the other things which followed.

My belief is that the purity of the channelling is greater after these cleansings.

The Polar Bear's Message

I saw a lone polar bear on the ice. It walked over to the edge of the ice looking for food in the sea. As I peered down into the water

136

with it, I was immediately struck by the curious green colour of the sea water. "Surely it should not be as green as this?" I thought to myself, and wondered if I was seeing it correctly. As I continued to gaze at the water, a seal swam up to the surface for air. I looked straight into its eyes which were full of worry and concern. The eyes seemed to be saying that something was wrong in the ocean. The bear caught the seal, fishing it out onto the ice to eat. I saw green water running off its body onto the white ice. I looked closely at this water seeing many little green things in it which were giving it its colour. I could not be sure if they were some kind of algae, or chemical pollutant, but they definitely should not be there I thought. The bear took a few mouthfuls from the back of the seal's neck, lost interest in eating it, and turning its back on the carcass gave it a disgusted half-hearted kick with a hind leg, and started walking away. I stayed beside the hole in the ice watching the bear as its form became smaller and smaller in the distance, until it joined one or two other bears in a far away place where there was more light. I looked around myself at the deserted empty ice flats, and knew that at one time there had been many bears living and hunting there, but this place was no longer able to support life.

The Elephants and The Animal Council speak to me

Two elephants were standing together holding each other's trunks affectionately. They spoke to me not with words, but through pictures. One of the elephants was larger than the other, and they seemed to be leading me to my second book, where they arranged themselves as a picture-to-be that they wanted me to paint for them just inside the front cover on the left hand page. This painting would be the first thing that people would see when they opened the book. It is an interesting point that it was the elephants who had given me some of my instructions about paintings for my first book. As I watched I saw a third elephant standing there on the left-hand side, and this was a baby elephant.

The largest of the elephants then picked me up in his trunk, and put me down on his back, where I sat astride to enjoy an elephant ride. All three of the elephants were coming, and as I looked round I saw that animals of all kinds were making their way through the trees on all sides of us. Eventually we reached the edge of a clearing where the animals chose to remain in the cover of the trees, and the big elephant wrapped his trunk around me and put me down on the ground beside him. I looked at the animals amongst the trees, and not having seen so many different species of animal gathered together for some time, I asked one of the angels, "What is this? The Animal Council or something?" "Don't ask us: ask them." an angel replied. Without further questioning, I found that I knew that it was the Council of Animals.

I did not stand there long, for I felt compelled to walk forwards on my own, and saw that there was a large camera on a tripod pointing directly at me from the centre of the clearing. I saw myself walk up to two people, one on either side of the camera, and shake hands with them. I felt that this meditation was part of my preparation for the interview with the Lhotsky Film Gesellschaft from Vienna that was to take place in Germany at the beginning of March. I assumed that this must be the microphone that an angel had handed me on 7th. January, 1994 in meditation. I felt a powerful energy force field, that held me in front of the camera, coming from the animals. A rather deep voice from one of the animals behind me rang out loud and clear, "We have brought you here. Speak for us girl!"

"You will have to tell me what you want me to say." I replied. Their message as I understood it goes as follows:

"We want to be respected as equal beings with mankind. NO LIFE-FORM IS SUPERIOR TO ANOTHER. The animals amongst us who are less well liked such as scorpions, or widow spiders are to some extent carrying and manifesting the shadow-side of consciousness which is a service to the rest of us, as we are relieved of that task, for we can observe it in them. The quality of the intellect is not a good measure for assessing the quality of the consciousness dwelling within each species. All consciousness is part of the SAME SOURCE, including that in the plant and mineral kingdoms. There is much to be learnt by men from observing the animals. There are a few animals who will kill for sport, but most hunt in order to feed themselves and their young. After that, even the most tender tasty morsel is left alone. The animals understand interdependence. None are self-sufficient. To exist on the planet, physical nourishment to sustain them is necessary. This is part of the system. Consciousness supports consciousness. Nothing is lost or wasted. Most of mankind is out of touch with the system."

Then I was shown a large tree with a strong and solid trunk, and deep roots reaching down into the earth. Each branch ended not with leaves, but with a species of animal. One branch supported mankind, who did not seem to know that they were sharing the same food source, the same sap drawn up from the earth by the roots of the tree as every other living creature on the planet, that they are part of us, as we are a part of them. This tree symbolised the simple fact that everything that exists on this earth and in the Universe came from the same source of consciousness, is part of the same Great Spirit, Light, Source, God, call it what you will. It was a tree of life.

After this meditation I had an overwhelming feeling that I would be able to do what ever was necessary during the documentary film interview. It was like an inner knowing that when the moment came, the words would be given to me. This feeling was reinforced when I discovered a dream that I had dreamt in March of 1986 neatly written out in an old notebook.

The dream was this. I was in a large hall, the centre of which was clear of people. Along one side of it were lined up a group of artists. I stood along another side in the audience as we waited expectantly to see which of the artists would perform first. I spotted a man with three balls which were the colour of pale blue light, and he was about to begin juggling with them. Intrigued, I leant forwards to get a better view. In the next instant I became aware that I had the balls, and was starting to juggle with them successfully. I had no idea how to do it, it just happened, as though the necessary movements came to my body automatically.

At the end of the act, I found that the balls had merged into one object which looked like three balls stuck together, and I could balance this where and how I wished, yet I still had neither knowledge nor confidence. After this, the artists took me among them to participate in the next act in which I was to sing. They told me what the tune was, but as we were about to begin, unable to remember it I asked in panic for someone else to start the singing, but no one else would. The curtain rose, and the split second before we began, the forgotten tune returned to my head, so I sang successfully.

Someone seemed to be telling me that worry and nerves were a waste of time, and that on every occasion when I really needed knowledge or help, it would be there. Trust!

Meanwhile, on the physical plane, the people from the film company "Lhotsky Film" had asked if it would be possible for me to paint a picture of the whole of the Council of Animals. It was quite clear to me that even with vast amounts of helpful inspiration and a lot of good luck, there was no way I could successfully paint all of them in one picture. I did, however, paint twelve of them. I knew that I was desperately short of confidence for the coming interview, and looking at this painting with the supportive energy field coming from the Council, who remained behind me in the trees, was very comforting. I used an artist's license, and gave the camera a remote control cable so that I would not have to try and paint the film crew who I had not even met! It meant that I did not have to worry about making them pretty enough, and avoided the risk of offending any of them. Painting people I find very difficult!

My Horse Wilderness

By now, I felt that the half hour meditation must surely be reaching an end, so I put the question silently to any entity who might be listening, "Is there anything else that I ought to know?"

"You ought to know who is looking at you." Immediately I saw Wilderness looking directly at me. He had light round him, and a beautiful white light above his head, only just above his alert ears. I was shown a small pair of scissors, which I knew meant that I needed to cut the psychic tie that was binding us together. I was reluctant to cut myself off from someone whom I loved so much, but had to trust that the advice that I was getting was good, and reluctantly I took the scissors, and cut the connecting energy line. Wilderness turned his beautiful head to look at something else, so I sent him blue light for healing, hoping that he would not suffer from a sense of loss, as I knew from past experience when doing this with people that the other person, although he or she may have no idea what has happened, may sense a loss, and try all the more desperately for a time to hang on to the person who has chosen to cut the tie.

The following morning, just as I was waking up in bed, the first thing that I was aware of was Wilderness standing in the far corner of his box looking dejected. He was missing the link. I made a note of that, and did my best to comfort him when I went to the stables later in the day. From my point of view, I found that I had a clearer perspective on the whole of my life, instead of only managing to see the bit of it that was centered round Wilderness. I understood that when I was too deeply connected or tied to him, that I lost touch with the other things in my life, that I tended to get emotionally out of balance. Meanwhile, I love him just as much, and he is looking happy again.

Chapter 21

The Pig's Story and the Mermaid's Message

The pig's story started when I was trying to paint the white arctic fox in the picture of part of the Council with me and a camera. I had been working at this picture off and on for the best part of two weeks, and I thought that I had painted all of the animals necessary for it. As I looked at it critically, I became filled with the awareness that there was yet another animal that wanted to be shown appearing from behind a bush on the bright green grass. "I wish I had known this earlier." I thought to myself as I tried to wash some of the green grass paint off the paper with a wet paint brush, so that I could add an arctic fox. I was anxious that the animal would not have the misfortune of being a pale grass-green instead of white.

I knew that the fox wanted to come, but it was really a struggle trying to stop it from looking like a little pale pink pig. With certain modifications, eventually the fox energy became dominant even if only just. There was nowhere in this picture where I felt I ought to paint a pig, so I declined to add one.

Before retiring to bed that night, I chose to put some music on and dance to the candle light. I knew that after sitting still for so long painting, the movement would help me to feel good physically before going to sleep. I had not been dancing for long, when I became aware of the energy of a large sow, at first on her own, and then with a family of piglets suckling from her. She began to talk. I sensed deep distress in her kind, and knew intuitively that it was the intensive pig farming, and lack of respect that most pigs have to endure from humans in their lives that was the cause of this. "But why?" she was saying. "What have we done to deserve to be treated like this? What did we do to the humans that they treat us this way?" My heart bled for her. I realised that she had been trying to reach me while I was painting the fox, but I did not hear her, just the energy came through my brush. I will paint another picture specially for her.

The Mermaid's Message

As I started to meditate, it was the birds who arrived first. They were all different, and with lovely markings and colours. They were twittering away, and in the following moment I had one perched on each ear pecking gently at my head around my ears. I felt that they were trying to further the development of my clairaudient receptors, or activate them a little, and a little blue-tit on top of my head was trying to stimulate my crown chakra with its beak. I was beginning to understand that the animals, having selected me for reasons beyond my present compre-hension, were doing what they could to assist my development into a good channel for them. There was a little robin sitting nearby. Robins often come close to people I have noticed. I found its presence comforting.

A mermaid appeared in the middle of all this. She was sitting on a rock, and clearly knew that I was worrying about whether or not my paintings would be good enough for the second book, and if they were not good, then I would have to disappoint the T.V. documentary film crew, who seemed to be pinning such high hopes on my abilities, by having nothing nice to show them. "Just enjoy the colours," the mermaid advised, and showed me gorgeous shades of blue and turquoise, which I could contrast with heaven knows what other colours. I was pleased that she spoke to me about it, as it made me a little less anxious, and a little more confident.

She held a champagne glass in her hand, and finished drinking whatever it was that she had in it, so that just a piece of fresh lemon was left at the bottom. I knew that she worked with the Animal Council, and that she was trying to show me that they

were already celebrating something. My feeling is that she wanted to communicate the joy that would be experienced on other levels when I took the step to speak openly in front of a camera, for she knew that this was only a beginning. More opportunities to help the animals this way would follow.

Chapter 22

The Animal Council and My Identity?

Both the mermaid's message and the story in this chapter took place on 13th. February, 1995, which was only two weeks before my trip to Germany to be interviewed by Lhotsky Film.

Obviously the animals were hoping that this event would help them, so it was hardly surprising that they were starting to visit me in greater numbers with increasing frequency.

Usually during these meditations, I either go through the whole experience without a body, or else I take one with me (a non-physical one), but the body seldom has any clothes on it. This is never a conscious choice, but simply how it happens.

This time I was wearing clothes, and I seemed to be at a very great distance from the reality of life as Helena on Planet Earth. An aspect of myself that I did not know about looked at me (through the eyes of the body I was in) and astonished exclaimed, "What am I doing in these clothes?!!" I looked like a normal human being wearing normal everyday clothes, but the aspect of me which spoke was not merely horrified by the clothes, but also by the human body inside them. It was like culture shock. "How did I get here?!" was the unspoken question. I felt so deeply shocked to be in a human body when the part of me which spoke clearly did not think that I was a human, that I looked across at the countless species of animals in search of my true identity.

I moved out of the human body that I felt so uncomfortable with, felt the link with the animal consciousness which somehow seemed closer to mine than the dreaded human identity, but could not decide which animal I was. I was looking for my own kind, those with whom I belonged. I wanted to be with them so badly, and I felt so lost. The animal consciousness was the nearest thing to it around me, even though I felt that I was not that. A kindly elephant allowed me to move into his body to try that one out.

Thrilled to be inside it, I went straight for the nearest tree and pushed it over so easily. It was wonderful having that much strength. The tree lay prostrate on the ground, its leaves now accessible for elephants to eat. "Just like cutting a lettuce." said the voice of the elephant in my ear, as I saw the similarity between a human going down the garden to harvest the salad from the vegetable patch for lunch, and a hungry elephant knocking a tall tree down in order to reach the leaves at the top of it when other food was not available. I became aware of the telepathic and physical contact between family members, but was much more interested in this amazing physical strength that was so new and exciting.

My immediate reaction was to look round and see what else I could knock over and destroy. I was not left in the elephant's body for very long. I expect I was too destructive, but it had given me tremendous joy. I do not think that I managed to get more than half into the consciousness of any of the other animals, but as I investigated the physical and mental qualities of several, tiger, monkey, scorpion I think, and one or two others (but unfortunately I forgot which ones too quickly to write it down before the memory was gone,) I found that each had something that gave me a different and free-er form of self expression, and I took great pleasure in expressing myself in ways that I have not been able to as a human. I wish I had not lost the details, but I learnt from this experience that the animals have things that are very special. They are unique and beautiful, each kind bringing its own particular gift to the planet.

After seeing and experiencing some of all of this wonderful diversity, puzzled, I asked "Why did I choose to come as a homo-sapien?" The reply came that they were the most out of harmony with the rest of life and the planet. Secondly, as a human I would have the freedom to move around and heal/help the animals. I would have a part to play in inter-species communication, and helping to heal the rifts between the different manifestations of consciousness.

This tells me a great deal about my purpose in this life, and I can see that I still have a very long way to travel.

This completed the meditation, but had time not run out, I felt that I could have sat there in the dark (the candle had gone out) thinking through what had happened for hours.

In the days that followed I thought about this meditation often. I was puzzled by the choice of content, and wondered why I had had these experiences. My surprise at finding myself in a human body with clothes on it seemed to be telling me that I was even less human than I thought, but what purpose did it serve to discover this? I knew about many of my extraterrestrial lives already, and also that I have lived many human lives before, and I thought that what mattered now was learning how to enter deeply into the experience of being a human, and how to enjoy this kind of existence in a physical body equipped with a complete range of human emotions on Planet Earth to the full.

I tried to see how this culture shock experience in the meditation had helped me. The feeling of being in a body that was not my rightful heritage had led me to look for another, so I had tried out several of the animal bodies to see if they felt any better. What did I discover? I had experienced first hand some of the unique qualities that the animals bring to this planet. One can say that some of them exist in limited degrees in mankind as well, but each animal brings something special to the planet. By letting me share their bodies and consciousness, albeit only for a very limited time, they were able to show me some of their uniqueness. It was this that I would need to share when speaking for them.

Chapter 23

The Teufelsteine, and the Wolf Who Did Not Know That He Was Free

This is a story that is two stories. One of them is the tale of a place with large boulders and three trees, and the connection between this place and the stories about it and the soul of a lone lost wolf. The other story is my account of my time in Germany in early March of 1995 for my interview with the Lhotsky Film Gesellschaft from Vienna with the intention of providing material for their film, helping the animals, and promoting the sales of my first book. The two stories become one.

Their film was to be about animals, and along with eight other people, all of whom had something special to offer for it, I was to be interviewed. Not only was this the first time that I had been interviewed, but I had no previous experience of how films were made, and the whole procedure was completely foreign to me. Therefore I was extremely grateful that Eva-Maria and Georg Lhotsky turned out to be two very friendly and easy to work with people who I really liked, as this made it easier for me to give them my best.

I was not completely sure what they expected from me, but I had the impression that to some extent they were willing to go along with whatever happened, and that they would be especially pleased if I could channel the animals for them on film. Although I was going to be there for two days, the first of these two days would mostly likely be taken up with the filming of two of the other people. So it happened. This was a great help to me, as I was able to watch a large part of it, and while watching I observed how the film crew of eight worked together, became a little familiar with the jargon and acquired an idea of what it might be like when my turn came the following day.

There was also time on the first day for me to be driven by Daniel (one of the film crew) to the site of the "Teufelsteine", where I was to be left alone to attune myself to the energies there, and decide whether or not this was a suitable place to be interviewed.

Daniel did not know this area of Germany, so it took us some time to find the "Teufelsteine". Therefore I had ample opportunity while we were travelling to think about everything. I pondered over the name "Teufelsteine". Literally translated it meant "Devil Stones", but as it had never crossed my mind that we would ever contemplate channelling the Animal Council, or any of the higher energies in a place connected with the Devil, I wondered if perhaps one could translate it into English as "Standing Stones". On the other hand, Eva-Maria, who told me that they had visited this place the previous evening, was clearly a little unsure about the energies there, although she had not entered into the middle of the stones, as she felt that it was a place where perhaps one should ask for permission before entering.

I wish to state here that I do not believe in the existence of the Devil. I can accept that there is evil, that there are bad energies and corrupted souls, but not the Devil.

With this almost total lack of information, we finally arrived at the Teufelsteine near the small village of Haiden. I went forward alone to make my personal psychic assessment of it all, while Daniel took the practical step of acquiring information by reading a public notice about it.

The stones were situated in a small clearing in a wood, and they were arranged like a figure of eight. In the centre was an old tree closely flanked by stones almost leaning against it. Then in one end of the eight were two more trees.

I remembered how in the Findhorn garden I had been capable of noticing the energy field carefully erected by the fairies for the purpose of keeping me and others out, therefore I was confident that if anything like that was present here, I would be able to feel it. The energies in this place were very different from the surrounding area. I noticed exactly where they intensified. I did ask permission to enter which was granted, but I do not know by whom. As I stepped into this energy field, it felt like moving back through aeons of time into another age. Time moved more slowly then, and everything was bigger. This is how I felt it. As I moved around I touched the various stones, and experienced some kind of closeness to them. You could call it love. To reach the tree in the centre it was necessary to climb up onto the bigger stones, and then I could lean against it and touch it as much as I wanted to. Immediately I began to tune in, I felt the tree's sense of security there. It felt safe surrounded by these stones. It knew that it was far too interesting a tree for anyone to seriously consider cutting it down. It was held in place and upright by the stones. I felt the connection between the tree and the stones. It was as though they were all part of the same family. When I touched the other two trees, it seemed that they happily shared the same energy and relationship with the centre tree and the stones.

I stepped back to the area just a little outside the stones. What would the Animal Council think of filming me in this place with all these ancient energies? I could see the animals, but instead of coming in close to me, they were still quite far away, and did not seem to like the place at all. At this point I was deciding that I must tell the Lhotskys that the Council did not like it, and we must do the filming somewhere else, even though this was definitely an interesting place.

Before leaving, I looked to see if there was anything else that I ought to know about it. I perceived this was like a pore in the surface of the Earth where the Planet could breath. Energies were moving into the Earth centre and also out from the centre of the Earth. I looked at these energies, and it was like looking at the air in sunlight when it is full of dust. I saw it as though the atmosphere was full of dirty smuts. I decided that a 'clearing' was a good idea. (It would be equally accurate to call it a 'cleansing', as it is simply clearing away the negative things in the atmosphere, which is the same as giving it a 'cleansing' or a 'clean'). I called the Elohim Angels (mentioned in chapter seven) to help me. They formed a circle round the whole area, and together we made a column of light in the centre. The smuts of negative energy were moved upwards into the light where they could be transmuted into positive energy. Anything else negative in the environment was invited and encouraged to use this shaft of light as an exit point from this dimension. I did not see any lost souls leaving, just the dirty atmosphere.

While this was going on, out of the corner of my eye, I saw a wolf running through the wood. It never looked my way, so I assumed that it had not seen me, and I felt certain that this particular wolf was nothing to do with the Animal Council.

I noticed a change in the energies. Everything felt less congested, and the Earth was breathing with greater ease. The 'clearing' was working. The energies were starting to flow more freely. I did not think that this cleaning-up operation was finished, but I did think that we were rather short of time, because we had had such difficulty finding this place, and therefore I ought to leave.

While driving me back, Daniel shared with me some of the information that he had read about the Teufelsteine while he had been waiting for me. Some weeks later Eva-Maria sent me a copy in German that she had made of the written version, so my own account which follows should be reasonably accurate.

There are two explanations offered.

The first version is that these large boulders (predominantly granite and deorite) form a prehistoric grave from the Neolithic Age, 4000-1800 B.C. These massive stones were brought from Scandinavia to Western Europe by the glaciers of the Ice Age. When the ice melted, these boulders were left lying on the ground, and were later used by the Neolithic people to make this burial chamber. (Perhaps even as recently as 2000 B.C.)

The second version is a legend from the Christian era.

"Charlemagne (Karl der Grosse) was building his cathedral in Achen. When difficulties arose, he sought the assistance of the Devil, who agreed to help, and made a deal with him. The soul of the first visitor to the cathedral after its completion was to become his.

Charlemagne thought that he could outwit the Devil, so when the day of consecration came, instead of sacrificing a man, a captured wolf was released into the building. The Devil, blinded by greed, tore the soul from the body of the wolf, thinking that this was the first human visitor, before he noticed the deception. He planned his revenge, and gathered a sackful of boulders which he was going to use to destroy the cathedral. In Haiden on the road to Achen he met a cobbler's assistant, who was carrying sixteen worn-out pairs of shoes on his back to be repaired. The Devil, who was already very tired, asked him how much further it was to Achen. The crafty young man, suspicious of the Devil's intentions, answered, "I have come from there, and so far I have worn out sixteen pairs of shoes on the road." With a terrible curse, the over-tired Devil threw the boulders onto the ground. Since then, they have been called the "Devil Stones".(Teufelsteine)."

As Daniel told me these things in the car, my German was not good enough to understand all of it, but the word "wolf" really excited me, because I knew that I had seen the spirit of a wolf close to the Teufelsteine. I did manage to grasp roughly what the legend said had happened to it, but not the whole of the legend.

When we arrived back at the hotel, it turned out that the others, with whom we should have gone, had already left to look at two alternative places for filming the following day, so having rushed back, I found myself with free-time which I gratefully used to go for nearly two hours walking in the woods.

While I was walking I kept on thinking about the story of the wolf. Could it be that the wolf whom I had seen was the spirit of the same wolf? If it was, then it must be a lost or an earthbound animal soul, and it needed 'clearing', that is helping to find its way into the light. I decided to call both the wolf and the Elohim Angels. At the same time, I put my hands on a silver birch tree. I chose a big strong one with plenty of life-force, and asked the tree to help supply additional energy for the work that I had in mind.

The wolf appeared just in front of me, very close, looking straight at me with open mouth, his tongue a little to one side slightly hanging out, and an expression of great attentiveness. The angels surrounded us with their wonderful supportive energy and presence. I asked the wolf what he was doing. Why was he still here when his life in a physical body took place so long ago, and he no longer belonged here. "Why don't you leave and move into the Light?" Without any words from him, I could sense that he thought he was stuck. By way of further explanation he showed me his chains which were binding him here. This was his way of telling me that it was not possible for him to go anywhere. "Oh dear!" I thought, "He is living in a non-physical state, but he still thinks that he is held here by physical chains, even though his chains are non-physical, and just something in his own imagination." I told him, "You are in chains because you think that you are in chains. If you did not think that you were in chains, then there would not be any chains, and you would know that you were free."

The wolf looked disbelieving at me. "Could this possibly be as you say?" was the question in his mind. I had spoken to him with great conviction, for I knew that I spoke the truth. The angel presence provided a comforting re-assurance for him, and after a while he was brave enough to take another look at his chains, only there were no chains there now. It was like a spell that had been broken. Free at last, he was ready to listen to my advice about using the shaft of light that was still present at the Teufelsteine. This would be like a gateway for him to leave the Earth and move into the Light for healing and rest, and with help to prepare himself eventually for what ever future or further incarnation would be best for him. His self-image was not good. He felt that he was unloved and despised, and that even the Devil rejected him for being a mere wolf instead of a man. I told him that he had given his life to save that of a man, even though the decision had not been a conscious one, and that after such a noble act he deserved a better future than he was presently allowing himself. He thought about all this for a while, and then found the courage to move towards the Light. I watched as he entered the bottom of the light shaft, and as he began slowly rising upwards, I knew that he would now be all right. Once in the light, his coat colour changed from a dreary grey to a lighter shade of grey that shone. It could have been just the light shining on him that made his colour change, but he looked beautiful. I thanked the birch tree and the angels, and moved on.

That evening in the hotel, I related this wolf story to the Lhotskys who were very interested. We discussed it all over dinner, and when debating how much truth there might or might not be in the legend, Eva-Maria pointed out that perpetuating the legend kept it in people's thoughts, and that the power of thought to create and influence is very real. Therefore it seemed reasonable to me, that if the spirit of a wolf who had died from natural causes was wandering lost through the forest, and then came into contact with the thought forms of this terrible tale of the Devil and the poor captive wolf, it could easily become confused and entangled

154

in this nightmare of a legend, only to be discovered at a later date by me as a prisoner in chains still on the Earth plane.

Both while walking in the woods, and during the night, I continued with the clearing of the energies around the Teufelsteine, for I knew that I had never really completed this work when I was still there physically, and also that it is not necessary when a link has successfully been made to take my physical body with me for this work.

Having gone to bed with the conviction that the Animal Council did not like that place, and therefore it would be much better to do all of the filming somewhere else, I awoke in the morning with an overwhelming certainty that it would be right to return to the Teufelsteine, and that this was what the animals wanted. So first thing after breakfast, I whispered in Eva-Maria's ear that if it were possible, I would like at least some of the filming to take place there. Actually I think that they had already decided that this should happen because of the wolf story. I suppose that I could have objected, but the animals would have been very disappointed. So after a brief visit to an alternative site which I did not like very much, I suggested that all of my interview could be filmed at or close to the Teufelsteine. This seemed to be pleasing to everybody.

When we arrived at the Teufelsteine, it was bitterly cold, and the filming had to take place in between snow flurries and passing aeroplanes. As I retold the story of the wolf, and answered various questions, I observed a noticeable change in the energies round these stones. Therefore I was no longer worrying about picking up dark energies, but found myself enjoying the increased amount of light. The shaft of light was still in place so that any lost animal spirits would be able to use it. As I sat on one of the stones with closed eyes, I saw many animals coming out of the trees attracted to the light. I knew that they would not have come before. Most of them were deer, and creatures of the forest. At one point, I was asked to tune into one of the larger stones, that is talk to it, so that I could be filmed in an alpha brain wave state. It would not be enough to pretend. It had to be real.

When I closed my eyes, I felt moved to do something different. After all, I had already spoken to the stone. So although I was standing there with my hands carefully placed on it, with my inner eye I looked upwards. I realised that I was standing in the very centre of the shaft of light. Immediately above my head, and high up was a wonderful place of light. Around this were many angels, and a circle of light blue around the white light. While part of me reached upwards to this beautiful place, I was also aware of light energy moving upwards through my body, the very same light energy that had transported the wolf to another dimension the previous evening.

Next I perceived that the angels were directing a strong light energy downwards which entered my body through my crown chakra. By now I was in a very altered state of consciousness, and I knew what was required of me by my unseen friends. Allowing this light to enter my being, I then consciously channelled it out in all directions through the whole of my body surface, throwing out my aura as wide and far as I could at the same time. While in this blissful state of being, I just managed to dimly hear the German command for the camera to stop running, as this was the end of that take. I withdrew my hands from the stone, and managed to walk out of the circle. I felt very spaced out, although not so badly that I could not speak after a moment or two. I stood there mentally growing roots into the ground to try and earth myself. I explained to Eva-Maria that I had really been somewhere, and I was still trying to get back. She told me that while they had been standing there filming, something had really hit her. This was most probably the channelled energy. Her testimony was very helpful to me, as it told me that this was not mere imagination, but something real that had happened.

Chapter 24

Wilderness

I have written a little about Wilderness in my first book. He is my beloved horse. At the end of Chapter four, I explained that direct communication with animals still incarnate on the Earth is seldom a part of my repertoire. This chapter and the following one tell of a few exceptions to that.

I knew that many of us have difficulty hearing what our animals say to us, because our telepathic receiving mechanism is poorly developed, so after listening to the animal communicator Kate Solisti talking about, and demonstrating her work in October, 1994, I asked her to talk to Wilderness for me. The things that he told her, and the things that he said he wanted made such good sense to me that I was convinced that the communication had been real. Next I had Trudi Hills come and work with him to help him with his body. Trudi was very skilled at mind to mind communication, so now Wilderness had found two people with whom a two-way dialogue was possible. It is my belief that this encouraged him enough for him to decide it might be worthwhile to see if he could talk to me. I am much harder to reach than either of these other two, but I will share the things that he did get across to me.

It was around Springtime in 1995 when I had been using Tellington-Touch and other 'TTEAM' work (as taught by Linda Tellington-Jones) to help his body, and on this particular day had concentrated on his neck to help him turn his head in a more relaxed way so that he could feel more comfortable. Wilderness had been feeling rather irritable throughout, and I felt he might have preferred it if I had left him alone and in peace. I changed my mind about this when I was driving home. I was just negotiating quite a tricky bit of road, when I became aware of Wilderness trying to communicate with me. He spoke in pictures, which is the language I understand the best. I saw that he was standing in his box experimenting with the movements of his neck that I had patiently been teaching him. It felt new and different, and he seemed to be asking me, "What is this?" Actually I was so astonished that I never even considered the possibility of giving him any kind of answer, but I remembered having read that sometimes horses do react like this after TTEAM. It starts them thinking, and trying things out.

Another time, I did not receive anything so specific from him. This is what happened. I rode him one day in the winter when the weather was really bad for man and horse alike. It seemed kinder than leaving him bored and under-occupied in his box. Unfortunately the endless rain had made the ground where I rode him very deep, so his work was much harder for his body than I wanted it to be. I put him back in his box, and then hurried away to help someone else with another horse elsewhere.

Very soon after I had left, I felt a deep depression coming over me. I was really in abject misery, yet I could not really rationalise it. My car journey took just under forty minutes, and as soon as I arrived at the other end, I jumped up onto the back of another horse to ride it for the owner. About two minutes later, my depression lifted. I felt happy again, even though it was still winter, and it was still bad weather. I carried on cheerfully, and forgot about the low spirits that I had been experiencing.

The following day, when I arrived at the stables to ride Wilderness, one of the girls who worked there had a story for me. She told me how only two minutes after I had driven my car out of the stable yard the previous day, Wilderness, who was feeling tired, and had not been looking very happy, had got down in his roomy box to roll, but did so too close to the wall, so got himself cast. ('Cast' means stuck, so that he could not get himself back onto his feet.) He lay on the floor in distress for a full forty minutes before, with the encouragement of the stable staff, he finally worked out how he could get himself far enough away from the wall to be able to stand up again. At last he relaxed and felt happier, and began to eat his hay. I saw immediately that the timing of the heavy depression that I had felt the previous day coincided exactly with Wilderness's time in distress on the floor. We were connected to one another.

Most horses have a weakness somewhere, and with Wilderness, it has always been his back. Therefore it is very important to look after his spine. He also feels the cold, so I keep him as warm as possible in Winter by putting rugs and blankets over him, which then need to be made secure, so that if he sits down in the night, they will not fall off when he gets up. Concerned about the pressure put on his spine by the roller (traditional type of belt to put round a horse's middle to keep the rugs on), I decided to supply him with the newest and most comfortable design of horse clothing that would avoid this problem. I left him looking very smart in his beautiful new blue horse-rug with lovely red binding round the edges, thought how happy he would be, and went home.

At about 11.00 p.m. as I lay in bed, I received an S.O.S. from Wilderness. He wanted to sit down, but as he began to lower his hind-quarters to the floor, the straps securing the new rug around his hind-legs, moved and tightened slightly, touching him where he was not used to being touched by straps. Horses are often nervous animals, and not knowing what the straps were going to do to him if he lay down properly, he was afraid. The old rug had not had any straps just there. I could see his hind-quarters trembling with fright as he tried to lower them to the ground. At that point I had not understood what was wrong, so I watched with great anxiety wondering if he was ill. Then to my enormous relief, he made it to the floor successfully without frightening himself any further, and both of us were able to relax. Much relieved, Wilderness broke the communication with me, for his little emergency was over. I knew that he was intelligent, and that having survived sitting down in his new clothes once, it would not be a problem the second time, and I went to sleep.

His next cry for help came about six months later. With autumn bringing lower temperatures, I had just started to keep him warm with a rug again. Unfortunately, because he was shedding the fine hair of his summer coat, and starting to grow the longer hair that nature provides him with for the winter, his skin was feeling very itchy. It seems that the rug on top was making it harder for him to scratch himself, so that he began to feel more and more irritable and bad-tempered as the night wore on. He wanted me to come and take the rug off, so while I lay in bed many miles away, in the early hours of the morning, he connected with me. He was really angry, and made a grab at my chest with his teeth. "Wilderness!" I screamed at him reproachfully, "You know you are not allowed to do that!" I had been lying there so peacefully, that I resented this ill-mannered intrusion, and at that stage, I had not managed to work out what exactly the problem was. Wilderness was really upset by my reaction. He had clearly hoped for my sympathy, not my anger, and had felt that he had to draw my attention to his discomfort somehow. He turned his back on me, and appeared to be sulking. I still had not worked it out, and lay in bed wondering if he was trying to show me that he had an itchy tail. Then the communication broke, and I went to sleep.

The next morning when I went to the stables, I discovered that he had torn his rug to shreds! At last I got the message, and managed to find him a rug that would keep him warm, but would not irritate his skin so badly while he was changing coat . ("Oh dear! These humans are so slow!" is what I would have thought if I had been him.)

I have mentioned how his back is his weak point already. Saddle fitting can be very difficult with some horses, just as others seem to be able to carry a well designed saddle very easily. Poor Wilderness had not been easy to make comfortable, so I had worked my way through various saddles to try and solve this problem. I knew that he was uncomfortable in his back somewhere, because he had communicated this to me through his behaviour. I could tell which movements he was finding uncomfortable to perform while wearing a saddle. If a willing horse does not want to co-operate, there is usually a good reason for it.

That day I had adjusted his saddle differently in the hopes of making it better, and too late I realised that I had given Wilderness a miserable time, as what I had done caused the saddle to pinch his spine more rather than less when he moved. So he had suffered for the whole of that ride, and I felt awful about it. I had caused him pain which he did not deserve, and why did this poor animal have to suffer so every time that I did something stupid? I lay in bed that night feeling upset about it, and went to the angels to ask them for help. I wanted some way of learning about life for myself that would not cause suffering to my horse. An angel was holding my hand, and I noticed that Wilderness was also there, but standing a little distance away from us. He was very attentive, and I saw a lovely golden light over his head, and also a blue light on his forehead. The angels showed me with a white arrow exactly which part of Wilderness's back was getting too much pressure. The following morning when I examined his back, I found that the place that the angels had told me about was slightly inflamed with a little swelling, but I was able to adjust the saddle panels to remove the pressure from this place before putting the saddle back on him. Later I managed to call the saddler who made it even better, and Wilderness rewarded us by working better and more willingly, and by giving us the enormous pleasure of seeing him look happier again.

Many times since then, when I have been thinking about Wilderness, I have seen him watching me, his ears moving to and fro as he listens to my thoughts. For this reason, I tell him many things such as "I am going away for five days, but then I will come and see you again." There are a number of stories that I could tell that suggest to me that he really understands. I would doubt that he knows the English language, but think it more likely that he somehow picks up the concept of my words in some other way, and certainly sending him pictures is a help. Telling him the truth seems to be very important. When I told him that I would be back in about five days, but due to bad weather, it took me about nine days to return, he expressed his disgust with bad behaviour in his box, which started the day after I had said I would be back but was not. Since then, If I am going to be late, I send him a telepathic message. My belief is that Wilderness is better at understanding my messages than I am at understanding his, although it is important that I make them clear, and stick to things that he can understand.

Chapter 25

Llum

Llum is a cat.

I have already mentioned that Sergi Aynó wrote letters to me after reading my first book. When I realised that this was to be more than just one letter, and that we were destined to meet each other, I became very curious, and I wanted to be able to picture in my mind how this man looked. Therefore when I wrote my second letter to him in December 1995, I asked him if he could send me a small photograph of himself.

With Sergi's third letter came the photograph, but there were two of them in the picture, Sergi and his cat "Llum". I could not see Sergi's eyes, but Llum had been looking straight at the camera when the picture had been taken. When I looked at Sergi, I felt very little, because his energy seemed to be either staying inside him, or else moving towards his cat. I was not sure. On the other hand, when I looked at Llum, she seemed to be almost jumping out of the picture to meet me. I could make eye-contact with her, and through the photograph I sensed a very strong feline energy which seemed to be reaching out in my direction. This was a surprise to me. I had not thought that I would be interested in a little cat whom I knew nothing about. I decided to put the matter out of my mind.

In early February (1996) I had planned to go to London where I would meet Sergi, and attend his 'Dolphin Workshop'. I was to arrive in London two days beforehand, so that I would have time to visit someone in a clinic about a fifteen minute walk from my sister's house, and knowing that I would have some free time after my appointment, I decided to telephone my sister, and ask her if I could visit her for a little while that morning. She explained that she did not want to see me, because even a short visit would be too tiring for her, and she 'had a lot on' the following two days. I had not seen her since my mother's funeral, twenty months previously, and the time before that was at my father's funeral in 1988. This alone made me feel very sad, but far worse than all of that was that her health had deteriorated very badly since I had last spoken to her. She was ill with multiple sclerosis, and for the first time in my experience her voice was quite badly affected by it. The exhaustion, and the desperation that I could hear in the tone of her voice reminded me of how my mother had sounded shortly before her death. I had difficulty holding my tears back on the telephone, when I felt that it was not a good moment to cry.

For the rest of that evening, I was so busy doing things that I managed not to think about my sister very much, and stayed fairly cheerful. As my mind quietened towards bedtime, it became harder. By the time I was in bed I was sobbing uncontrollably. I am quite comfortable with tears, and feel that grief is better expressed than held inside, but it was preventing me from sleeping, and I felt that I must somehow manage to feel happy enough to stop crying and sleep, so that I would be well rested before tackling the following day, but how?

When I feel unhappy and alone, I often start thinking about other people who may also be suffering, and wonder how it is for them. My mind went to Sergi's little cat. Sergi lived in Spain, and now he was in London. I did not know that the cat was happy living with another cat staying with Sergi's parents, so I wondered if it was alone in Sergi's house feeling abandoned. My heart went out to it. The next thing that happened was that I saw a cat approaching me. The cat appeared to have come out of water, for it looked very wet. "Hello! Who are you?" I asked. Immediately behind herself, so that it appeared that she was walking out of it, she showed me the picture of Sergi and herself. "Is that you? Are you Sergi's cat?" I inquired."Yes, I am she." came the reply. Llum continued to approach. Still wondering if she had been feeling lonely, I told her that I liked comforting beings who are left alone, or feeling sad. On reaching my bed where I was lying on my side, she lay down and curled up into a ball just in front of my tummy. At this point, I began to really look at her aura. It was like a soft golden light, and as she lay there, this light began to expand until both of us were enveloped by it. Something remarkable happened. I felt my sadness being taken away from me. It was replaced by a wonderful sensation of wellbeing. I knew that it was Llum who was doing this for me. I thanked her. I think that she was temporarily taken away from me by some other energy, but not for long.

Although I cannot prove it, my belief is that she returned later that night while I was sleeping, and that we went on a long out of the body trip together somewhere. Llum is the last thing that I can remember before I went to sleep. My body was warm and comfortable, but at 5.00a.m. I woke up, and my feet (and especially the right foot) were like ice. They were still in my warm bed, but I know that if I am out of my body for too long, even under many blankets, first my feet, and then gradually the rest of my body will start to lose heat until it is really uncomfortable with the cold by the time that I get back into it.

I was able to meet Sergi for the first time the night before his workshop when we had dinner together in London. I told him the story I have just related, but I forgot to mention that Llum appeared to be sopping wet. Sergi, however, completely spontaneously told me the story of how he found her. It goes like this.

One day when he was staying with his parents, Sergi decided to go for a long walk up into the mountains where there was a very big tree under which he wanted to sit down and read his book. This favourite tree was quite close to a river, and as he was approaching the tree, he noticed something floating in the water that looked like a little animal, perhaps a mouse or a rat. A few minutes later he saw another little something floating down the river, and then quite soon afterwards a third little something. This time he had a very strong feeling that he must go into the water. He took the little creature out of the water, and saw that she was a little kitten. There was still some blood from the umbilical cord, so she must have been born that very day. The other little animals were probably her brothers or sisters, and were already dead when Sergi saw them, having been thrown unwanted into the river by the owner of the mother cat. The little kitten in Sergi's hands was only just alive. The sky was overcast with clouds, but Sergi held her in his hands, and intuitively offered her life to the sun. At that moment, as he prayed for her life, the clouds parted just enough for a ray of sunlight to shine through them onto the tiny kitten's body. He felt that the sun healed her. Therefore he called her "Llum", which in Catalan, his native tongue, means "Light". That was 19th. September, 1987.

Quite soon after seeing Sergi in London, at the request of Pilar Baste who had just published my first book, I went to Barcelona to give a presentation talk about it. Although I had had a smooth and uneventful flight, I was really over-tired, and the combination of mental stress and flying, had left me exhausted, and I was not at all comfortable as I lay in bed that night. My body did not feel good. The room was peaceful and quiet, so it was easy to notice when I had company. Llum came. Out of her body again! She did not need to make herself visible, as she started to purr. Although the sound was coming to me on another dimension, the vibrations from it started to heal my body until I was comfortable. It only took a few moments, and then I was able to sleep. Not surprisingly, my interest in this cat was growing! I asked Sergi if anything like this had happened with him, as I felt that somehow she must be looking after him. This is the story that he told me.

Sergi has had a number of 'out of the body' experiences. When these have occurred, leaving his body has been spontaneous and without his conscious control, but he can usually control his return. On one occasion he arrived back to find that there was a problem re-entering his body. It felt impossible, and he knew that something in the room was not right. He became aware of something that looked like a red light. Although it was not possible to see if this was another entity wanting control of his body or not, he sensed that the energy with it was not good, and that this was the reason for his difficulties in reentering his body. He also saw that Llum was there. Llum stood in front of the red light and hissed at it. This kept it distracted for just long enough for Sergi to be able to use that moment to get back into his body.

Back at home in England again, I could not resist sometimes stopping to look at Llum's picture. One day, as I was doing exactly that, I felt her coming towards me again, as though she were coming out of the photograph which of course must carry her vibrations, and acts like a connection to her. My surprise was that I spontaneously found that my mental body (less dense than the astral, and my usual means of out of the body transport) moved forwards to greet her. My idea was that when we met I wanted to stroke her with my hand, but I had no control, so I started to lick her. She in turn was licking me.

After about two licks, I noticed that my tongue had grown smaller, and changed its shape and texture. My next surprise was my body. For the first time in this life, I found that I had a cat's body. I was really inside it, and this meant that I could relate to Llum as a cat would. I licked her, and I rubbed my face and my body against hers, and she returned my attentions. I was just the same size as her. I even climbed over her in much the same way as a kitten might when playing with another kitten. Perhaps this was the only way that I could come so close physically, for Sergi has told me that she is normally very afraid of allowing people whom she does not know to touch her, but when I came as a cat... it was different.

By this time, I was absolutely certain that Llum should be a chapter of my book, so I telephoned Sergi to ask for permission, and also to make sure that I told these stories accurately. We checked through the parts that concerned Sergi, and then I asked if there were any more stories that he could add. This is what he told me.

Before he had Llum, there had been a time when he owned a rabbit. Unfortunately the rabbit, who had to live in an apartment that he was sharing with a friend, was very fond of chewing and eating the furniture. This was seriously upsetting Sergi's friend, so the rabbit had to go. Sergi gave it away to someone he felt would give it a good home, but felt that he had betrayed the trust of his little furry friend, as the understanding between them had been that they would always be together. Sergi was left with strong feelings of guilt, which he was unable to let go of.

When Llum came into his life, he knew that someone had abandoned her, and that she must have known that she was unwanted, so he promised her during the first year that he had her that he would be with her for ever, that he would never leave her. Occasionally he had had to go away for the week-end, but had always managed to leave her in his flat with someone else coming in to feed her for the two days. Then the time came when he had to agree to go to Germany for two weeks, as he was still working as a dancer. He was very worried about leaving Llum alone, so he arranged with his parents that she would go to their house while he was away, and they could look after her.

While in Germany, Sergi suffered terrible feelings of guilt. He felt that he had broken his promise with a second animal. The guilt seemed to feed the negative emotions of both guilt and fear. Therefore he decided that he must telephone his parents not only to ask how they were, but also to ask after Llum. The parents were in good health, but Llum was really very ill, in fact so close to death that they told Sergi that if she was not better by the following day it might be the kindest solution to have her put down rather than leave her to suffer.

Sergi was very upset. He could not forget that at the time when he had rescued her from the river, the people living around him then told him that it was a big mistake to try and nurse Llum back to full health. They told him that she must have taken too much water into her body ever to manage a complete recovery, and that it would have been kinder to let her die in the river.

These memories added to his feelings of guilt when his parents told him how much she was suffering. Instead of losing hope, he decided to try and help her. He spent about an hour sitting on his bed communicating with her telepathically. During this time, he not only spoke to her, but he also sent her his body smells so that she could feel his presence. He told her that although he was not with her physically, he was still with her, and that he would always be with her.

The next day he telephoned his parents again. They asked him, "What has happened? What have you done with her? She is perfectly healthy and normal again. She has been playing games with the other cat!" They could hardly believe it.

Sergi pointed out that this had been the first time that he had been away for so long, and also the first time that she had had to live in another house, so she must have really believed that she had been abandoned by him. Also Sergi's own emotions, he believes, had affected her very negatively, that is his fear and his guilt. I would add that just as I had felt so unhappy and depressed when Wilderness was cast in his box, and lying there in distress and misery, even though I knew nothing about what was happening, it is only logical that Sergi's state of mind should have affected his cat, for they too were connected to each other. There were many reasons why I needed to visit Sergi, and one of them was that I had never been with Llum physically. Intuition told me that two days would be the right length of time to resolve the main issues, and eventually we managed to find mutually convenient dates.

Sergi had told me how Llum did not like anyone other than him to touch her, so when I knew that I would be spending some time in her space, I decided to communicate with her telepathically, so that when I arrived, it would not be so difficult for her. I told her that I was coming, and that if she was there I would see her. Inspired by Sergi's story, I sent her my body smells. She was very interested, and I experienced her sniffing my body. One day when she came, I forgot that I was in my human body, and, because I loved her, I reached out to stroke her. She was horrified, and shrank back from me. I told her that I was sorry, and promised to respect her wish not to be touched in the future. Clearly, one either had to be Sergi, or approach in a cat's body.

When I arrived at Sergi's house, her wish not to be touched had not changed, but she was very interested in smelling me in exactly the same way as she had done when out of her body. There was some two-way telepathic communication between us. I noticed that she used her energy to assist with Sergi's "Dolphin Healing Sessions", as when I received one of these, there was a moment when I was very conscious of her auric field enveloping me, and giving me a wonderful sense of well-being.

On another occasion when I was alone in the room with her, and she knew that I was just thinking how beautiful she was, and not "I would like to touch you," she decided to throw out her aura until it surrounded both of us. The love in it really touched my heart. On two occasions she sent me pictures to let me know what she was doing, or where she was going. I was always very aware that she could read my thoughts.

I feel that Llum has really opened a door for me, and that although I have a great deal to learn, she was helping me with inter-species communication.

Chapter 26

Helena E.T. and Sergi Dolphin

Llum was not the only reason for my visit to Sergi Aynó. I have already told the story of my past life as an E.T. when I met dolphins in the ocean, and shared the consciousness of one of them for a while. I have also said that both of us felt sure that he was the dolphin in my life and I was the E.T. who had connected with him so closely. More convincing than the comparison of our two accounts were our bodily reactions to the renewal of our deep friendship of long ago. Sergi had felt a rush of energy surging up his spine as he started to read the first of my letters to him, and when I opened one of his letters my cells began to recall his vibrations, and I was covered in goose-bumps which lasted for ages!

Then there was ease of communication. With 'strangers' I usually only want to show my good side. With Sergi I wanted him to know everything. I wanted nothing to be hidden from him. I wanted to regain the level of honest intimacy that we had shared when he was a dolphin. From deep inside me the knowledge that this is the only way that my soul knew in which I could feel at one with and really comfortable and relaxed with another being was coming to the surface. It would be untrue to say that I was totally free from fear and anxiety, but I did notice that when I shared personal things that were difficult, I had no fear of rejection or judgement. Even at the beginning of this renewed friendship I felt safe. Sergi told me that usually he had difficulty in expressing himself at the beginning of an acquaintance with someone, but not with me. Why?

So it was in March 1996 during this visit to Premia de Mar, near Barcelona that Sergi, who had not read Chapter 14 (although it was already complete), asked me if I would be willing to help him take another look at his dolphin life, as he wanted more information about it. Although I thought my profession was teaching people to ride horses, I had had some training from Rhea Powers in this other type of work, and when at a later date I had helped a friend's daughter look at two of her past lives, I had been surprised to find myself going into a light form of trance when I was too nervous to manage on my own, and gratefully allowing another being to use my body and voice to get the session started. When I had recovered from my nerves, the other entity took a step back, and I came forward to carry on with it, knowing that in the case of difficulty, someone who could help was very close behind me and inspiring me.

I reasoned that if another entity whose presence I had never consciously asked for had helped me once, then perhaps I would be helped again if necessary. Therefore I agreed to be Sergi's facilitator in this, having first explained that it would neither be a "Rhea Powers Session", nor a "Light Institute Session" (I had never had any training from the Light Institute), but a "Helena Session", for I worked with the help of inspirers in what ever way felt right at the time.

Sergi's Dolphin Life

In the session, we moved backwards and forwards through time seeking the most important information, but to make it easier to read, I am putting it back into chronological order, and including all of the most relevant material.

Sergi was born into a large pod of dolphins in the Atlantic Ocean 25 degrees north of Ecuador. These dolphins had a special mission. They were the keepers of a "City of Light" which existed in another dimension very close to the third dimension, and of which the dolphins were aware. This city contained crystals in which was stored the whole history of Planet Earth, and the dolphins' work included checking the energy balances there.

As a baby dolphin, as well as swimming around with his dolphin mother, Sergi found himself putting his nose into a special crystal (from another dimension) as he wanted to receive information from it, but the crystal said "No. Not now, but in the future." The other beings who lived in the City of Light came from the Earth, but were in the same dimension as the city. They were able to communicate with beings from other planets, but as a dolphin, Sergi did not find this unusual.

Sergi was female, and mated with one of the males. Mating was an ecstatic experience. He (she) did not feel any emotional dependency, but loved the male very much. The same was true the other way round for the male. Sergi became pregnant, and his attention was with the baby inside his womb. There was a feeling of dependency, but it was with the whole pod, a caring for each other.

The dolphins knew that the Earth must change, because the people living on the land were not living in the right way with the planet. Far away on the land they could hear explosions, and there was fire. The people there were manipulating power. The majority of them had power, and the others were working for them. They experimented with different mixtures of various gases and chemicals, and as a result of this, one day there was a particularly violent explosion. The dolphins started to swim away from it as fast as possible, but Sergi was nearly ready to give birth, and did not have the strength to keep up with them, so he became separated from the rest of his pod.

The pollution that the explosion had caused was preventing most of the sun's rays from reaching the Earth.

These events left Sergi very worried. This was not a good time to give birth, because he wanted his baby to be born in the sunlight. Therefore he gave birth alone, and close to the surface, as there was a little light in the sky. The baby was female. He helped her to breath out the first time, but was much more relaxed when she was able to do it for herself.

He wanted to find the rest of his pod, but he could not. So he found himself swimming around in the dark with his baby feeling very worried. He could not see any fishes, and he knew that they needed to eat. He decided to swim out into the middle of the ocean, as with the explosions, it was too dangerous to stay near the land.

Far away from the land in the depth of the ocean, with his sonar he detected a space-ship that had life in it on the ocean floor. His sonar informed him of the life-forms inside this ship or space-capsule, although he could not see them. He perceived that the space-people were strong beings, but gentle, and immediately felt safe with them. As a dolphin, he was not surprised to find them there, and he told one of the entities that he and his baby needed to eat. They sent out a special sound through the water which attracted different species of fish. A few seconds later there were a lot of fishes around, so Sergi and his baby were able to eat. This was the beginning of a friendship.

Sergi still could not see the shape or bodies of these E.Ts., but he appreciated that they were helping him, and he could feel their strong presence very easily.

The E.Ts. were checking the marine life in the oceans of the Earth planet. Close to the space capsule was a deep dark hole in the ocean floor, and they wanted to explore it, but they needed sunlight to help maintain their energetic systems, so they were reluctant to go down there for very long, as it could have resulted in their death. Sergi offered them his support by sending sounds to help them know where exactly the darkness began. This was important for them, as they had kept their capsule in the same place for many days, and they needed to move it, but not into the hole!

Other dolphins arrived, but from other pods, not his own pod. Sergi was able to join them, and they too began to work with the E.Ts. The dolphins played together, and ate fishes.

Sergi described how he could feel that these beings were able to swim beside him and over him. One of them seemed to be hanging on to him as he swam, (This was Helena E.T. we found out later in the session.) and although afraid of the darkness, it felt safe with him, and seemed to be enjoying it as Sergi swam and played in the ocean. I queried this point after the session, because I considered that I had been inside him, not hanging on to the outside. Sergi said that part of me had been inside him, but he perceived that part of me was outside him as well. This seemed to fit very well with my own memories of it, for I knew that my aura would have extended well beyond the boundaries of Sergi's dolphin body.

While this was happening, Sergi saw that there was a red light flashing in the space-ship which meant that part of my consciousness could not function in the capsule at that time, because it was out in the water with Sergi. The space-ship was small, about two or three metres across. After the session Sergi told me that its colour was amber, or bright orange. This was very interesting, as that was the main colour of Base Planet, and Sergi still had not read Chapter 14! (I had sent him a copy of it, but it had found its way to a neighbour's house, and Sergi did not receive it until after my visit. This turned out to be very fortunate, as it meant that there was no possibility of Sergi trying to make his story fit with mine, although he did know that he had linked up with me when he was a dolphin.)

The presence of our space capsule is not something that I had been aware of in my Light Institute session, as I remembered the return trips to Base Planet without the need of a vessel when we needed to recharge our energy systems, but the accuracy of the colour (Sergi had not been told what our colour had been) convinced me that the information was as close to accurate as is possible when trying to describe with words things from other dimensions.

More dolphins arrived, and a lovely reciprocal friendship was formed between the dolphins and these beings.

Sergi Dolphin died a natural death when he was old. It was a blissful experience as he moved into a state of light. It was ecstatic.

The message at the end of the session from Sergi's Higher Self was that the purpose of this life had been to learn about inter-species communication with beings from other planets and those living in different dimensions, and learning to forgive those who are working on this planet in the wrong way.

I have met several people who remember their lives as dolphins, and nearly all of them are now concerned with helping us renew our connections with this species, and in teaching us how we can allow the consciousness of the whales and the dolphins to remind us who we are, and to allow them to help heal us.

Sergi is no exception to this, as in many different countries he is currently involved in helping people to have their own dolphin connections in his workshops and dolphin healing sessions, and activating cellular memories, thus helping people to remember that we are cosmic beings. I experienced one of his dolphin healing sessions as particularly effective in the healing of my emotional body.

Chapter 27

And Finally...

My Inner Life

This was a beautiful meditation that came to me on 3rd. April 1995 when meditating at home with my friend Margot.

I found myself kneeling in front of a small pool of water. I looked in it, and saw my own reflection with the sun smiling, and the moon paler and less obvious, and observed that there was an angel standing behind me.

After I had had a good look at all this, the angel led me by the hand through some trees to a place where I saw a ray of light that reached right down to the Earth from a distant star. We stepped onto the bottom of this ray, and were transported upwards in a way that reminded me of riding on an escalator.

The star was less dense than Planet Earth. There were creatures there of the same density as the planet. I saw what looked like a large fly with beautiful rainbow colours in its wings. There were also vaguely bird-like beings flying about. In fact it was a little like a flying school for spirits who were accustoming or preparing themselves for life in matter. I was allowed to experience it for myself, although not in insect or bird form. I flew around in this atmosphere of energy particles of many colours. My form (body) had no bones or anything rigid in its structure, which meant that I was very pliable, and of no fixed shape. The colours that I was experiencing were mostly metallic, bright, clear, and beautiful. Everything was shining and reflecting light. I needed no wings to fly with. Just wanting to was enough to bring it about. I was able to fly through all of these coloured particles, which were also transparent, and as I moved, I could feel resistance from them against my changing form, rather like moving through water, and yet quite different from that. There was no gravity as we know it on Earth. Therefore all directions were equally easy to travel in. I flew in smooth graceful lines enjoying the sensation of moving through the particles. One side of this planet revealed its interior. I saw it as though the shell had been removed on that side, and its centre of strong pure white light was accessible to me and the other beings living there. It was as though we belonged in the middle of it, but the atmosphere around it was the training ground for flying.

Taking my hand once more, (at that point I was in a body that had a hand!) the angel led me on, and I understood that it was time to visit another place. This next place had many angels, and was full of light. In the centre of the scene that I was observing, I saw the back view of a coloured man holding the hand of his little son. The skin of both was very black. The two of them stood quite still there while the angels attended to them. Neither of them wore any clothes. One of the angels in particular seemed to be doing something with the light around the man's head. It could have been some kind of healing, but I only knew what I saw. When they left the angels, I followed them back to some primitive looking wigwam type of dwelling on Planet Earth. I surmised that they visited this place of light and the angels when they were in their sleep state.

Somehow following them back to the Earth seemed to bring me back to this dimension as well, and I sat there wondering at how it could be that people from such a different and far away culture could be found in the same place as me when out of their bodies. I thought that their needs would be so different, that they would visit different places, with different angels. My surprise about this is really the only puzzling part of it. I remember past lives when my skin was black, or even other colours that were not white, and yet I was the same being, and was never under the impression that my skin colour or nationality affected where I went at night in my sleep. I knew all that. So maybe it is some triviality like geographical distance, or the way in which society conditions us to think about other cultures that had caused my reaction.

The Council of Animals have told me so many times that it is important to understand that the animal kingdom is neither superior or inferior to the humans, for we are all from the same Source.

The angels were reminding me how this is also true of the many different peoples on the Earth. We are the same.

And Finally... A Word from The Ascended Masters

This came on 4th. May 1995, once again when I was meditating with Margot.

As I sat there in my chair feeling very tired, and having difficulty with concentration, I realised that whether or not anything happened in this meditation was up to me. The angels were there ready to do something or go somewhere with me if I wanted, but I was under no pressure to make the effort. I expressed my willingness for something, and waited to see what that would be.

We began walking. First we went through woods following an uphill path, then climbing still higher beyond the trees we reached a beautiful place where the rock formation reminded me of the famous Pinnacles on the Welsh mountain Crib Goch. These pinnacles (in my vision) were in a place with a mystical quality, and very beautiful. Having been washed or cleaned up in some way in so many of my previous meditations by the angels before going to higher places, I had the feeling that I was not in a fit state to progress further without some sort of clean-up, so I started to draw lilac coloured light in through my crown chakra and then through the whole of the rest of my body like a cleansing water to purify myself.

Almost immediately I started this, the angels began to pour a shower of golden light over me, so I had their cleansing as well.

After this, we took off upwards into the atmosphere, and it was not long before we arrived at a place where I saw the Ascended

Masters assembled in a circle. I drifted around in their midst. It seemed right for me just to be there absorbing the vibrations and becoming part of the scene. When I was ready, the Masters manifested a round table in the middle of their circle. On it was a pile of books. I wondered if these could be my books, the first one, the second one, and the ones that I have not yet written. I looked at them and thought to myself, "In each of those books everything is perfectly arranged. Just the right amount of the right things in the perfect order and the paintings must be correct in number and flawless. Will I ever manage to bring all of this through to the Earth with that much perfection? What an awesome task!"

Much to my astonishment one of the Masters stepped forward, and with a single sweeping movement of hand and arm, he sent the lot flying up into the space above us where the pages separated, and, each one a different pretty pastel colour, they fluttered gently downwards to land on Planet Earth. They were so much a part of me, that I found myself drifting down with them, aware that each contained a message destined for the Earth. As we landed, the pages and I, and before I could really start to contemplate how I would ever manage to put them back together arranged in the perfect order, I saw one of the Ascended Masters in front of me coming towards me. It was obvious to him that I was worried about the books, as he said,

"There is no need to take it all so seriously!"

His face was full of joy and love, and I received from him something that was like a hug, and yet he was not close enough to hug like a human. It was more of an 'energy hug'. He seemed to wrap his energies around me for a moment, which gave me the sensation of being hugged and loved, and yet there was nothing in the way of physical contact, or use of the arms.

This wonderful being understood me down to the very last detail. He knew that I am normally very critical of myself, and that especially lately I have judged myself as under-achieving. When comparing my life with those of other people, I think that I manage very little in the time available to me. This leaves me thinking that I am inadequate, or lazy, or allowing life to slip past me without making good use of the time. Other people manage to earn more money because they work harder, etc. etc..

With great clarity the Master advised me,

"You are looking at yourself with the eyes of the World. It would help you to look at life from a different angle. See how working on yourself, and being filled with light alters the way in which you touch other lives and everything else around you with that light."

This made things look much better. I could see my perspective on life starting to come from a much more peaceful place, and become less contaminated with the materialistic views of a consumer society.

I felt very greatly comforted.

The above communication was of such value to me, that it was enough for one evening, and during the remainder of the meditation time, I rested.

Epilogue

The Nine Paintings, and Conclusions

The Nine Paintings

I have to speak of these. Two of them were done in time for Lhotsky Film to see them in 1995, and the rest of them many months later. This time I have signed them with my initials. On the one hand I cannot take full credit for them, but on the other hand I cannot hold the animals themselves or any other sources of inspiration responsible for what ever imperfections these pictures may have. This is because I am not able to go into a full deep trance, brush in hand, and wake up an hour or two later to view a completed picture that I know nothing about. Instead I spend time studying the subject/animal, time meditating and asking for inspiration, and then hours of work fitted in before and after my part-time work with the horses struggling (I think that is quite a good word for it) to try and get them good enough. The wolf picture took eight or nine days of this. Obviously I had completely forgotten the words of the Ascended Master mentioned in the last chapter, "There is no need to take it all so seriously!" because I even had bad dreams on one occasion in which I made a horrible mess of one of them! It was a relief in the morning to wake up, run down stairs, and discover that it was not as bad as I had dreamt.

A few things happened on their own, which was interesting for me. For example with the elephants at the beginning of the book, I was not happy about how the grass was growing. Suddenly I understood. Of course the grass near the water would be longer, as it was growing near water!

I painted the physical aura of the hedgehog, as it is a good thing to remember that animals have auras just as much as we do.

When I came to the owl, I was really worried that this was too difficult for me, painting a bird so large that details like feathers and eyes really had to be mastered. The eyes were important, because I had seen them so clearly in my vision, and the soul views the world through them. One morning on waking, with my inner eye I saw the owl looking at me as it sat in an oak tree. I could have mistaken this as merely my own painting, but the bird was opening and shutting its eyes to make me realise that it was truly present. I received the message that the bird consciousness was with me, and that I must continue to paint it. The following morning after another day of painting with all my doubts, the owl paid me another visit. This time I saw the tree-branch swaying up and down in the wind. It was as though the tree-spirit was saying, "Come on! Paint me as well!"

The spider was easier, as painting energy fields seemed to be a more natural process.

The background for the bear more or less happened on its own. I put colour where I felt it should go, and an impression of snow and ice appeared. The bear itself was harder work, but one night I saw bears walking around my bed giving me a feel of their energy to put into the painting. They were always moving with a sort of expectant restlessness, as though waiting for something, which I felt was more than the completion of the painting, for it came to me later that it was the publication of the finished book, and an increased state of awareness on the part of mankind that they were interested in.

After drawing some of the Animal Council with me and the camera, adding the energy field seemed a bit of a risk. It could have ruined the whole thing could it not? I would have had to start again from the beginning. A lesson in trust perhaps, but it worked.

I was out hill-walking worrying about my pig not making a nice enough picture. Besides, she looked so lonely all on her own. The rabbit came. "Put me in the picture," it said. So I have. After all, it was the rabbit who told me in my first book that I had to paint all of the pictures myself, and it said then that the animals would help me.

My first idea with the wolf was to paint it in the heart of a wood where I first saw it, but the night before I started on the background, I was given another vision in which I saw clearly the dark branches, perhaps even darker than I have painted them against the blue sky with the hills showing through the trees, which reminded me of the venue where I spoke to the wolf the second time. Therefore I changed my plan. The branches almost close in around the wolf, who does not seem to see the way out of the forest to his left any more than he could see a way out of this dimension into the Light.

The paintings were mostly painted out of order, but the dolphins were painted last. They had an interesting effect on the artist. Although I took great care to try and make the dolphins look like dolphins, and to let their energy come through, I was very aware that they did not want me to make hard work out of this one. It had to be fun, and it was. I saw in meditation that there should be three dolphins, and that movement and excitement were called for. Inspired by a story I have yet to tell in this book, I knew that there should be islands. After that the picture seemed to paint itself while I was playing with it as a child might play. I thought that the dolphins were going to be swimming in open water, but I noticed that actually they were in the calm waters of a small bay with an opening leading to the ocean.

I painted the clouds, and saw that one of them was a storm cloud that wanted to let its rain fall, so I painted the rain. I did not know why I must paint a storm cloud with rain. Sunlight was catching the hills on the islands, although not shining in the foreground. Why should these things be? A day or two after I had finished it, I learnt from a television documentary that there had been an ancient culture of people living in the Bahamas long ago who worshipped the twin gods of the Rain Spirit and the Sun Spirit, so the picture has the balance of both, and the dolphins are enjoying themselves. Two days later I discovered a brochure about a dolphin workshop in the Bahamas which had the information on it that in 1969 Edgar Cayce predicted that Atlantis will rise again near Bimini in the Bahamas. in the same brochure it was stated that the dolphins are said to be the guardians of the vestiges of the ancient civilisation. All this coming to me after the painting was complete! The connections will be clearer when you read Glenda Huggons' story in "Conclusions."

It is my wish that the paintings should add to the enjoyment of those who read this book, bring some of the energy of the animals to them, and also that they will help by acting as a memory aid to keep the messages of the animals in their hearts. I painted each one of them with love.

Conclusions

Long ago when I triumphantly typed the last words of Chapter 27, I thought that I had finished writing this book. About two months later my kind proof-reader Jill Robinson said words to this effect.

"Chapter 27 reads like a build-up to a climax. I was so excited, but when I turned the page over, there was nothing! You cannot just stop like that Helena! You must write some more." So I thought of an epilogue. It took time before I knew how I could tackle this. I had more material, but at least some of that belongs to Book Three which I have not even started to formulate yet, and the other things? Well, they do not belong here.

Listening to Jill's response to the rest of this book has been very helpful to me, as it made me think that I should include more of my own reactions to its contents. She described how where I had written of things of which she had had even the tiniest bit of personal experience, it was reasonably easy to accept them as fact. Whereas anything that was completely outside her present knowledge she had to put on 'hold' as she expressed it.

So now I will share some of my own reactions to the more unusual stories, for example my E.T. life in Chapter 14 where I describe all those planets, and my encounters with dolphins.

The further I went through that lifetime (lying flat on my back under a sheet on a table, and assisted by my Light Institute facilitator), the more I began to question it. The same fear that dreads the possibility that I 'might not get it right' and causes such anguish sometimes when I am painting was working very strongly in me at that time. There would be someone out there with far more knowledge who would be able to assure me that my imagination was running riot and that the true facts were actually very different. "How can I stop myself from making it all up as I go along?" I asked myself. "I will be ridiculed after this. I don't think I can cope with that. I am too sensitive." (I think that my ego felt threatened!) More thoughts came in, and luckily of a more positive nature. "If I am getting it all wrong, then I know no way of getting it differently. If I start trying to censor out the most unlikely bits it will stop the flow, and then I will not be able to get anything. This session is the most fun that I have had for a long time. I need not tell anyone else what was in it, so why not carry on just as I am and continue enjoying it?" How lucky I did!

There is still a lot in it for which I have not had any confirmation, but little by little more and more supporting evidence has come my way. At first, I put nearly all of it on 'hold' as Jill would say, but little by little I have been able to fully accept more and more of it. There was Sergi Aynó and his session described in Chapter 26 tapping into his dolphin life and his experiences with me as an E.T. Then while I was attending the Annual Dolphin Tribe Gathering I had an interesting conversation with Ashleea Nielsen who organised the gathering with Sergi, and runs the Dancing Dolphin Institute on Maui, Hawaii. We were relaxing in the swimming pool one afternoon discussing dolphin incarnations when Ashleea who knew nothing of the Sergi-Helena/dolphin-E.T. connection said, "Of course some people don't actually have their own dolphin lives straight away. They come and hitch-hike, as I call it, with a dolphin, and then incarnate as a dolphin after that." Following a little discussion, I realised that Ashleea's 'hitch-hiking', and Sergi's description of one of the E.Ts. "hanging onto me as I swam", and my 'shared consciousness' were all the same thing.

For me, this part of the story was definitely not on hold any more. I had too many reasons to believe it.

One might call Sergi's behaviour and purpose as a dolphin into question. One might ask the questions "Are dolphins really so intelligent? Are they as conscious and aware as these stories suggest?" My own memories validate a great deal of it, and then just as I was wondering what I could find to write about in an 'exciting' epilogue, I picked up the letter of a friend and healer, Glenda Huggons, and studied with interest what she had to say about her past life as a dolphin. I quote from her letter, "In previous meditation work I had been a dolphin at the time of Atlantis (or another lost continent) relaying telepathic messages across the water from one island to another." This gives further support to the type of dolphin intelligence described by Sergi.

I intuitively felt that this was exactly what I needed for my epilogue. If these memories had come to her during her meditation, I wanted to know more. I wrote to Glenda asking for permission to publish her story using her name if possible. She gave me a very quick and helpful response, so that although I was not ready to use her material immediately, over the following weeks my mind was at rest with the knowledge that it was there for me when I needed it. In order to give me as much information as she could, Glenda took the trouble to meditate again using the same dolphin meditation tape as she had used in 1990. This is what she told me.

The first time these memories came to her, she and twelve invited friends were all meditating together in a special room that Glenda used for healing and small group meditations. When they shared their information afterwards, there were some vague similarities in the type of content received. At a later date a psychic told Glenda that all of them had been in Atlantis.

Glenda was a bottle-nosed dolphin, and found herself with her head out of the water looking around. To the left and in front of her she saw what appeared to be an island, but her inner-knowing told her that it was actually Atlantis. Most of it was already under the water, with just the higher buildings looking like an island still reaching upwards above the waterline. They were clean and white with very simple architecture reminiscent of Greek Islands with their little churches. (In an Atlantian life of my own I remember white or light-coloured buildings with plain undecorated architecture, but there were one or two arches in the most important buildings. Like Glenda, I had seen no artists' impressions or films about it.)

Although only the buildings were visible, Glenda knew that she was a messenger, and that she communicated telepathically with humans as she travelled from island to island, or place to place carrying information. (Interesting, because I read in a book that before the white men forced the Aborigines to move away from the fertile coastal areas of Australia, they had found it possible to have "head-to head" communication with dolphins just as they did amongst themselves.)

Then came a vague recollection of sometimes having to make deep dives down into what seemed to be a paranormal kind of underworld to deliver her information. Glenda assumed that it must have been quite valuable information that was perhaps a little secret or sacred, as that was how she felt about it at the time. (Also interesting, as Sergi had told me in a letter that when he was in Kona, Hawaii, the dolphins had taken him down to a place in the water where there appeared to be an inter-dimensional gateway, but that he had been warned that it was not the right time to pass through it, although one day many of us would be able to.")

On the second playing of the dolphin meditation tape in late 1996 the story carried on as Glenda found herself in the exact same spot as the first time with her head out of the water bobbing up and down viewing the 'Island' of Atlantis. This time it seemed to be all about emotions. As the dolphin she felt incredibly lost and sad. She knew that Atlantis was no more, and was mourning the loss of human contact, and the loss of a role or "raison d'etre" for her. These strong feelings of bereavement were what she was left with as the dolphin energies around her gently and lovingly brought her back into this reality. Glenda was helped by these dolphin energies (of 1996) to see how that situation was affecting her life today, so that she could heal it. I find this wonderful, as it shows how other-life work is not an ego-trip, or merely an interesting bit of research, but a useful tool to help us live in the moment.

Now perhaps the connections with the painting intended to somehow help illustrate this epilogue are clearer. I had opened myself to inspiration as much as I could, and unwittingly painted a 'Bahama-like' location linked with the twin spirits of the 'local' Sun and Rain Gods, and which it turns out is linked in some way to Atlantis. Although I set out by painting the ocean my favourite shade of blue, I found myself moved and inspired to add a little green to some of the water, and as it happens the waters around the Bahamas are noted for their turquoise blue colour.

This is the end of Book Two.

My love to all of you,

Helena.

FREE DETAILED CATALOGUE

Capall Bann is owned and run by people actively involved in many of the areas in which we publish. A detailed illustrated catalogue is available on request, SAE or International Postal Coupon appreciated. **Titles can be ordered direct from Capall Bann, post free in the UK** (cheque or PO with order) or from good bookshops and specialist outlets.

Do contact us for details on the latest releases at: **Capall Bann Publishing, Freshfields, Chieveley, Berks, RG20 8TF.** Titles include:

A Breath Behind Time, Terri Hector
Angels and Goddesses - Celtic Christianity & Paganism, M. Howard
Arthur - The Legend Unveiled, C Johnson & E Lung
Astrology The Inner Eye - A Guide in Everyday Language, E Smith
Auguries and Omens - The Magical Lore of Birds, Yvonne Aburrow
Asyniur - Womens Mysteries in the Northern Tradition, S McGrath
Begonnings - Geomancy, Builder's Rites & Electional Astrology in the
    European Tradition, Nigel Pennick
Between Earth and Sky, Julia Day
Cat's Company, Ann Walker
Celtic Faery Shamanism, Catrin James
Celtic Faery Shamanism vol 2 - The Wisdom of the Otherworld, Catrin James
Celtic Lore & Druidic Ritual, Rhiannon Ryall
Celtic Sacifice - Pre Christian Ritual & Religion, Marion Pearce
Celtic Saints and the Glastonbury Zodiac, Mary Caine
Circle and the Square, Jack Gale
Compleat Vampyre - The Vampyre Shaman, Nigel Jackson
Creating Form From the Mist - The Wisdom of Women in Celtic Myth and
    Culture, Lynne Sinclair-Wood
Crystal Clear - A Guide to Quartz Crystal, Jennifer Dent
Crystal Doorways, Simon & Sue Lilly
Crossing the Borderlines - Guising, Masking & Ritual Animal Disguise in the
    European Tradition, Nigel Pennick
Dragons of the West, Nigel Pennick
Earth Harmony - Places of Power, Holiness & Healing, Nigel Pennick
Earth Magic, Margaret McArthur
Eildon Tree (The) Romany Language & Lore, Michael Hoadley
Enchanted Forest - The Magical Lore of Trees, Yvonne Aburrow
Eternally Yours Faithfully, Roy Radford & Evelyn Gregory
Everything You Always Wanted To Know About Your Body, But So Far
    Nobody's Been Able To Tell You, Chris Thomas & D Baker

Face of the Deep - Healing Body & Soul, Penny Allen
Fairies in the Irish Tradition, Molly Gowen
Familiars - Animal Powers of Britain, Anna Franklin
Forest Paths - Tree Divination, Brian Harrison, Ill. S. Rouse
From Past to Future Life, Dr Roger Webber
Gardening For Wildlife Ron Wilson
Goddess on the Cross, Dr George Young
Goddesses, Guardians & Groves, Jack Gale
Handbook For Pagan Healers, Liz Joan
Handbook of Fairies, Ronan Coghlan
Healing Book, The, Chris Thomas and Diane Baker
Healing Homes, Jennifer Dent
Healing Journeys, Paul Williamson
Healing Stones, Sue Philips
Herb Craft - Shamanic & Ritual Use of Herbs, Lavender & Franklin
In Search of Herne the Hunter, Eric Fitch
Inner Celtia, Alan Richardson & David Annwn
Inner Space Workbook - Develop Thru Tarot, C Summers & J Vayne
Intuitive Journey, Ann Walker Isis - African Queen, Akkadia Ford
Journey Home, The, Chris Thomas
Legend of Robin Hood, The, Richard Rutherford-Moore
Lore of the Sacred Horse, Marion Davies
Lost Lands & Sunken Cities (2nd ed.), Nigel Pennick
Magic of Herbs - A Complete Home Herbal, Rhiannon Ryall
Magical Guardians - Exploring the Spirit and Nature of Trees, Philip Heselton
Magical History of the Horse, Janet Farrar & Virginia Russell
Magical Lore of Animals, Yvonne Aburrow
Magical Lore of Cats, Marion Davies
Magical Lore of Herbs, Marion Davies
Magick Without Peers, Ariadne Rainbird & David Rankine
Masks of Misrule - Horned God & His Cult in Europe, Nigel Jackson
Medicine For The Coming Age, Lisa Sand MD
Medium Rare - Reminiscences of a Clairvoyant, Muriel Renard
Mind Massage - 60 Creative Visualisations, Marlene Maundrill
Mirrors of Magic - Evoking the Spirit of the Dewponds, P Heselton
Moon Mysteries, Jan Brodie
Mysteries of the Runes, Michael Howard
Mystic Life of Animals, Ann Walker
New Celtic Oracle The, Nigel Pennick & Nigel Jackson
Patchwork of Magic - Living in a Pagan World, Julia Day
Pathworking - A Practical Book of Guided Meditations, Pete Jennings
Places of Pilgrimage and Healing, Adrian Cooper
Practical Divining, Richard Foord
Practical Meditation, Steve Hounsome
Practical Spirituality, Steve Hounsome
Psychic Self Defence - Real Solutions, Jan Brodie
Real Fairies, David Tame

Reality - How It Works & Why It Mostly Doesn't, Rik Dent
Romany Tapestry, Michael Houghton
Runic Astrology, Nigel Pennick
Sacred Animals, Gordon MacLellan
Sacred Celtic Animals, Marion Davies, Ill. Simon Rouse
Sacred Dorset - On the Path of the Dragon, Peter Knight
Sacred Grove - The Mysteries of the Forest, Yvonne Aburrow
Sacred Geometry, Nigel Pennick
Sacred Nature, Ancient Wisdom & Modern Meanings, A Cooper
Sacred Ring - Pagan Origins of British Folk Festivals, M. Howard
Season of Sorcery - On Becoming a Wisewoman, Poppy Palin
Seasonal Magic - Diary of a Village Witch, Paddy Slade
Secret Signs & Sigils, Nigel Pennick
Self Enlightenment, Mayan O'Brien
Spirits of the Air, Jaq D Hawkins
Spirits of the Earth, Jaq D Hawkins
Spirits of the Earth, Jaq D Hawkins
Stony Gaze, Investigating Celtic Heads John Billingsley
Stumbling Through the Undergrowth , Mark Kirwan-Heyhoe
Subterranean Kingdom, The, revised 2nd ed, Nigel Pennick
Symbols of Ancient Gods, Rhiannon Ryall
Talking to the Earth, Gordon MacLellan
Taming the Wolf - Full Moon Meditations, Steve Hounsome
Teachings of the Wisewomen, Rhiannon Ryall
The Other Kingdoms Speak, Helena Hawley
Tree: Essence of Healing, Simon & Sue Lilly
Tree: Essence, Spirit & Teacher, Simon & Sue Lilly
Through the Veil, Peter Paddon
Torch and the Spear, Patrick Regan
Understanding Chaos Magic, Jaq D Hawkins
Warriors at the Edge of Time, Jan Fry
Water Witches, Tony Steele
Way of the Magus, Michael Howard
Wildwood King , Philip Kane
Wondrous Land - The Faery Faith of Ireland by Dr Kay Mullin
Working With the Merlin, Geoff Hughes
Your Talking Pet, Ann Walker

FREE detailed catalogue and FREE 'Inspiration' magazine

Contact: Capall Bann Publishing, Freshfields, Chieveley, Berks, RG20 8TF